2-

EVALUATING

E-Learning

Here Is How You Can

- Predict Success
- Measure Value
- Prove Worth

D1441593

ASTD
Linking People,
Learning & Performance

William Horton

Copyright © 2001 by the American Society for Training & Development. (ASTD). Reprinted 2003, 2004.

All rights reserved. Printed in the United States of America.

No part of this publication may be reproduced, distributed, or transmitted in any form or by any means, including photocopying, recording, or other electronic or mechanical methods, without the prior written permission of the publisher, except in the case of brief quotations embodied in critical reviews and certain other noncommercial uses permitted by copyright law. For permission requests, write to ASTD, Publications Department, Box 1443, Alexandria, VA 22313-2043.

Ordering information: Books published by ASTD can be ordered by calling 800.628.2783 or 703.683.8100, or via the Website at www.astd.org.

Library of Congress Catalog Card Number: 2001117681

ISBN: 1-56286-300-2

All figures are printed with permission of William Horton Consulting.

Contents

Preface

When I was nine, I sent away for a pair of X-ray glasses advertised in the back of a Superman comic book. The advertisement promised that I would be able to see through objects. To my disappointment, all I could see were halos of light around the edges of objects. It was a tough lesson about exaggerated claims.

As a young trainer, I came across a recommendation to intersperse short training sessions with naps for the students. The recommendation seemed a bit strange, but it claimed to be based on research and included the universal seal of approval: a bibliographic citation. After I tried the procedure and could not get it to work, I tracked down the article cited. It turned out that the article merely summarized research done elsewhere. So, I followed its citation back to yet another article, where I found that the trail continued. In this pre-hypertext era, tracking the recommendation back 12 jumps to its original research took five weeks and involved trips to three libraries. And, when I finally located the original article, I found it concerned research on cockroaches!

Today, when something promises to slice, dice, prevent acne, cure baldness, relieve indigestion, or guarantee instant riches, I subject it to "open-minded skepticism"—receptiveness to ideas that must prove themselves. In the wake of the dot-com financial shakeout, potential customers, clients, and investors for e-learning are joining me. Unless you are one of the tribe born every minute, some of the overblown claims made for e-learning should have you demanding proof as well. Appropriate skepticism is essential for the evolutionary success of good ideas. More good ideas are scuttled by the blind faith of their zealous advocates than by the whining chorus of their naysayers.

WHO IS THIS BOOK FOR?

This book is for people who are not satisfied with the Polyannaish claims of self-interested suppliers, consultants, and developers or the dire predictions of the neo-Luddites who fear technological change. It is for those who want to know whether e-learning really works. It is for those who want to know how well it works. And, it is for those who have to prove that it works. This book's audience may include anyone producing e-learning or considering buying e-learning, such as:

- training managers wondering whether e-learning makes sense
- team leaders of e-learning initiatives who must sell e-learning to their companies
- leaders of for-profit training firms who must sell to skeptical buyers
- HR executives concerned with balancing the costs of alternative approaches to raising levels of knowledge and competence
- people who want to know whether e-learning will work for them.

WHAT WILL THIS BOOK DO FOR YOU?

This book will help you make decisions about e-learning based on proven performance rather than vague promises. It offers simple, specific techniques to estimate costs and prove results. If you are considering buying e-learning courses, it will show you how to objectively evaluate the contenders and estimate their total costs. If you are developing e-learning, it will teach you to predict and document financial returns for your projects. If you sell e-learning courses, it will show you how to demonstrate objectively the effectiveness of your courseware to skeptical buyers. If you champion e-learning in your organization, this book will show you how to demonstrate its contribution to prized corporate objectives.

WHAT'S SPECIAL ABOUT THIS BOOK?

This book is your toolbox for evaluating e-learning. This book shows you a gamut of measures from smiley faces to return-on-investment. It is chock-full of examples, worksheets, and specific procedures. It is very action oriented. At the end of each chapter, "Your Turn" sections guide you in applying what you have just read to evaluating your e-learning project.

The book's companion Website (www.horton.com/evaluating/) contains spreadsheets, forms, and worksheets for analyzing the costs, benefits, and returns of your e-learning projects.

William Horton
September 2001

1

The Value in Evaluation

Does your e-learning work? How much does your e-learning project benefit your organization and your learners? Is e-learning a wise investment or a waste of corporate resources? And, how can you improve your e-learning efforts? Only an objective, accurate evaluation can answer these questions.

Evaluation means, literally, assigning a value to something. It answers questions about the value of your e-learning course or project. Evaluation teaches you about how well your learning solutions work and how you can improve them. This book shows how to apply proven methods to the task of evaluating e-learning.

WHY EVALUATE YOUR E-LEARNING?

E-learning projects have recorded some spectacular successes. These successes may suggest that your e-learning projects will work equally well. Reported success should encourage you but not convince you. As they say in the automobile advertisements: "Your mileage may vary," or, as is printed at the bottom of a stock prospectus: "Past results do not guarantee future performance."

First, realize that only successful projects tend to be reported. If a project was not completed, or if its failure would embarrass the sponsors, the project will probably not make it into the academic or trade press. And, even if other projects have succeeded, their success may not signify much for your project if it differs in substantial ways. You have different goals, face different problems, and rely on different resources. By the time you complete your project, the conditions that led to success in earlier projects may have vanished. Or, new technology may offer solutions to problems that stymied earlier projects. In any case, someone else's success does not benefit you. Only your success does that. *Only your evaluation can measure your success.*

SPECIFIC REASONS TO EVALUATE

Before evaluating e-learning, you need to be clear about why you are evaluating. Consider a few specific reasons to evaluate your e-learning:

- *Justify investments in training.* An effective evaluation can prove that training is not a net expense but a strong contributor to profit. Such proof can help training jump from the cost column to the benefit column in the mental ledger of top executives. Proving that training is an effective business investment spurs increased investment in training.
- *Make better decisions about training.* A proper evaluation process can aid in making informed business decisions regarding training, such as whether to buy, license, or build particular courses; whether to hire particular individuals or firms to develop training; which training media to use; and which internal and external suppliers to hire.
- *Hold participants accountable.* Evaluation reveals whether individual training departments, developers, instructors, facilitators, and suppliers delivered the results they promised.
- *Demonstrate financial responsibility.* Evaluation demonstrates to executives, stockholders, and employees that the training department is financially disciplined and clearly focused on the business goals of the overall organization.
- *Improve training quality.* Evaluation can measure the quality and effectiveness of various aspects of training, such as materials, instructors, facilities, and presentation techniques. It can identify areas that need improvement and ones that can serve as models of excellence.
- *Encourage learning.* The very process of evaluating learning focuses attention on results and encourages learners to try harder. Tracking job performance signals the importance of applying what was learned in training. The evaluation process may be more important than the data it gathers if it strengthens efforts to apply knowledge.

ANTICIPATE OBJECTIONS TO EVALUATION

For all the reasons to evaluate e-learning, there are as many concerns about evaluation, especially as commonly practiced. Though some objections to evaluation are ill informed, you should honestly consider them and be prepared to overcome them before embarking on the evaluation. All these objections can be countered with a carefully crafted evaluation plan. That's what this book is about. Here is a list of some of the common reasons for not evaluating e-learning:

- *Evaluation is too expensive and difficult.* Many training organizations believe they lack the budget, time, or skills necessary to mount an effective evaluation program without endangering their primary mission of conducting training.

■ *Results will be meaningless.* Many in training fear that all the effort of an evaluation program may be pointless as it is nearly impossible to accurately gauge the effectiveness of training. Some fret that benefits are too subjective and ephemeral to measure and that they take too long to accrue.

■ *Irrelevant factors dominate results.* Training can fail for reasons other than the training product itself. Real-world results have many causes. Many believe that it is too difficult to dissect out the effects of training. Anyway, e-learning is so new, much of what is measured will be the novelty effect.

■ *Evaluation is too political.* In a highly contentious organization, the idea of evaluation can set off political battles and organizational paranoia. Who sets the criteria? Who is evaluated? Who sees results? Instructors who teach in classrooms and managers who preside over large training facilities may feel threatened if evaluation compares e-learning to conventional training.

CHARACTERISTICS OF A GOOD EVALUATION PROCESS

This book will help you develop an evaluation process that works for the kinds of evaluations you need to perform. Before diving into the details, let's look at the characteristics of an effective evaluation process. It must be:

■ *Flexible, suitable for various forms of training:* An effective evaluation process should work for a wide variety of training projects. It should provide for evaluation performed at different stages of the project, for both technical and soft-skills training, and for both formal and informal training programs.

■ *Simple, easy to implement:* A good process is simple enough that everyone involved can understand it, that executives can trust the results, and that participants can carry it out. It is important to remember that evaluating e-learning is not a form of academic research but a pragmatic measurement of business success.

■ *Reliable, able to accurately measure or predict results:* At the end of the evaluation process, do you believe the results? Are they consistent from project to project (or are the reasons for the differences easily explained)?

■ *Economical, involving minimal costs:* A good evaluation process should have limited effects on budget, schedule, and staffing requirements of the project evaluated.

As you design your evaluation plan, strive to give it these characteristics.

YOUR TURN

At the end of each chapter, you will find suggestions on ways you can begin applying what you have just read to your organization's e-learning efforts. Most of these worksheets consist of simple questions with spaces for you to write your answers. If you are reluctant to mark up this book, you may want to download and print out copies of all these "Your turn" activities from the book's Website (www.horton.com/evaluating).

Why should you evaluate e-learning? Use worksheet 1-1 to identify some reasons your organization should evaluate its e-learning programs. Then, worksheet 1-2 can help uncover your objectives for evaluating e-learning.

Worksheet 1-1. Why should your organization evaluate its e-learning?

Reason to Evaluate E-learning	How Does it Apply to Your Organization?
Justify investment	Learner Population is diverse and dispersed throughout all regions. E-learning allows for training staff w/o travel cost
Make better decisions	Helps us understand what types of content are best for e-learning as well as what made a program successful or unsuccessful
Require accountability	Ensures that training content delivers what it says it will deliver
Demonstrate return-on-investment	See 1. but also shows it was successful w/o the overhead of ILT
Improve quality	Feedback allows for changes in future courses to correct issues (address)
Encourage learning	learners know the time investment and don't feel held hostage by instructor so they are more engaged

Worksheet 1-2. What are your objectives for evaluating?

List three specific objectives for your evaluation efforts for e-learning:

1.

2.

3.

Next, anticipate objections that your evaluation plan is likely to encounter within your organization. As you read the rest of this book, jot down on worksheet 1-3 ways to overcome each objection.

Worksheet 1-3. Be prepared to overcome objections.		
Objection	**Heard This?**	**How Will You Overcome This Objection?**
Too hard and expensive		
Results lack meaning		
Results are irrelevant		
Evaluation is political		

2

Perspectives of Evaluation

Before you can chart a course to a destination, you must first identify your starting point. For evaluating e-learning, that starting point represents your perspective on e-learning. It involves the breadth and depth of what you want to discover, your economic role and place in the development process, and where you want to focus your efforts for improvement.

BREADTH OF VIEW

At what scope do you want to evaluate e-learning? Are you interested in rating an individual course or in assessing the long-term effects of e-learning on society in general? Evaluations can range along a scale from microscopic to macroscopic perspectives (figure 2-1).

In the micro view, you are concerned with concrete results in accomplishing specific learning objectives. In the macro view, you are concerned with a broad range of results in accomplishing organizational and political goals.

Figure 2-1. Spectrum of evaluation perspectives.

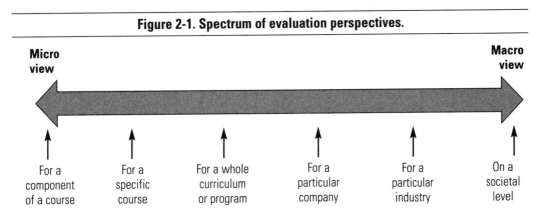

Micro view					Macro view
For a component of a course	For a specific course	For a whole curriculum or program	For a particular company	For a particular industry	On a societal level

Your Economic Role

Training cannot be evaluated in an economic vacuum. When you evaluate training, you do so from the viewpoint of your economic role. That role may be one of a producer of training, a consumer of training, or both (figure 2-2).

Figure 2-2. Evaluate, keeping in mind your economic role.

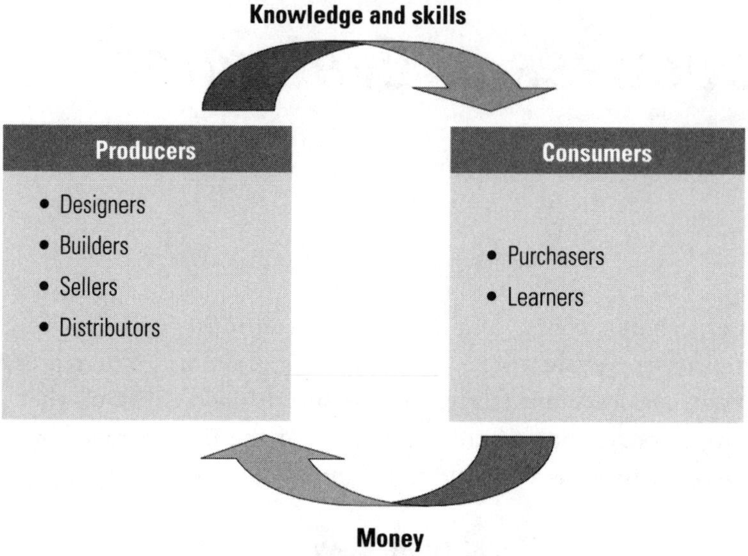

Knowledge and skills

Producers	Consumers
• Designers	
• Builders	• Purchasers
• Sellers	• Learners
• Distributors	

Money

Producers supply consumers of training with knowledge and skills. In return, consumers pay producers. Producers, therefore, are often concerned with the profitability of the exchange, while the consumers are more concerned with the effectiveness of the resulting training.

Within each main role are other groups with more specific interests and goals. Learners who do not pay for training themselves may disregard the fees or purchase price of the training. Nevertheless, they may be quite concerned with whether the training is convenient and entertaining.

Evaluating from the different perspectives of consumers and producers is covered in chapter 9.

Timing of Evaluation

When will you evaluate e-learning? Evaluation is possible at three main points in the development process:

1. before training is developed
2. between development and deployment
3. after training has been conducted (figure 2-3).

These three points use the same basic evaluation techniques but in somewhat different ways. For example, you can predict return-on-investment before

**Figure 2-3. Three points in e-learning development
that present opportunities for evaluation.**

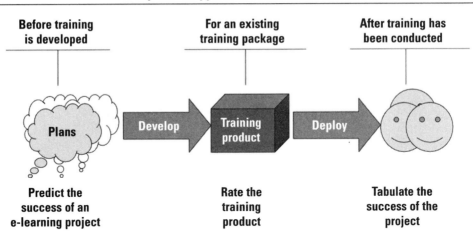

Before training is developed	For an existing training package	After training has been conducted
Predict the success of an e-learning project	Rate the training product	Tabulate the success of the project

the project begins. Then, at the end of the project, use the same process to compare actual results against those you predicted. These results can help you more accurately predict the success of your next development project or assess the value of an e-learning product you are considering buying.

INTERNAL VERSUS EXTERNAL EVALUATION

Evaluations can look inward at how you work or outward at what you accomplish. An internal evaluation aims at improving your development and management processes to make you more efficient. An external evaluation seeks to improve the results of your process as experienced by customers, that is, those who buy and take your training.

Though separate internal and external perspectives are possible, they are closely linked. Internal processes exist only to produce external results. Improving internal processes leads to better results, and knowledge of results provides clues for improving internal processes.

LEVELS OF EVALUATION

Most evaluations take a layered approach using the basic model developed by Donald Kirkpatrick (1996). This model is remarkably resilient. Though it originated in 1959 when computers cost millions and weighed tons and when the word "network" applied to television and not computers, this simple four-level model provides an able framework for evaluating e-learning (figure 2-4).

Starting with level 1, each level of evaluation measures more far-reaching consequences of training. Level 1, or response, evaluation gauges learners' immediate reaction to training. Did they like it? Did they even complete it? Level 2, or learning, evaluation asks how much participants actually learned. What specific skills, knowledge, attitudes, beliefs, or understandings did they

9

Figure 2-4. Kirkpatrick's classic four levels of evaluation.

Level of evaluation		What it measures
4	Results	How well did the organization meet its business goals? Was the result profitable?
3	Performance	How much is job performance improved? What can learners apply to their jobs?
2	Learning	What skills and knowledge did they acquire?
1	Response	Did learners like the training? Did they complete it?

acquire as a result of training? Level 3, or performance, evaluation measures to what degree learners can, will, and do apply learning to their jobs and lives. Level 4, or results, evaluation gauges the business results of training. Were business goals met? Was training a worthy investment of organizational resources?

You may have encountered one or more of these levels or used them. To put them in perspective, consider three characteristics: how commonly each kind of evaluation is performed, the difficulty of performing it, and the value of the results.

Few Do Higher-Level Evaluations

When ASTD (2001) asked training organizations about their use of the four levels of evaluation, the results showed a consistent trend across the three groups surveyed. The trend was clear: the higher the level, the lower the number of courses evaluated.

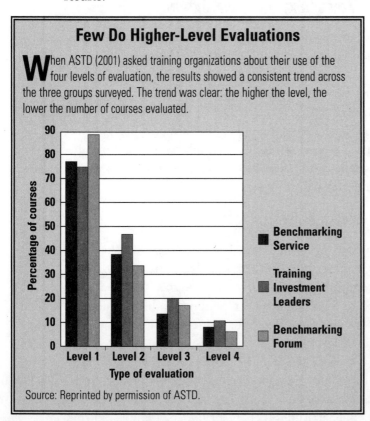

■ Benchmarking Service

■ Training Investment Leaders

■ Benchmarking Forum

Source: Reprinted by permission of ASTD.

Level 1 evaluations are quite common, perhaps because they are easy to perform. The value of their results, though, is low. As you move up through levels 2, 3, and 4, you find that the evaluations become less common, doubtless due to increasing difficulty and expense. Value, in terms of accurately assessing the full benefits of training, however, increases for higher-level evaluations. These levels of evaluation are the organizing scheme for chapters 3 through 6, which discuss how to perform evaluations at each level.

YOUR TURN

Your choice of evaluation strategies and tactics depends on your perspective on evaluating e-learning. Take a few minutes to explore that perspective with worksheet 2-1. Using the issues identified in this chapter, describe the perspective of training evaluations currently performed by your organization. What perspectives should you take in evaluating e-learning?

Worksheet 2-1. Analyze your perspective on evaluation for e-learning.

Perspective	Positions for Your Evaluation	Why Evaluate From This Position?
Breadth of View At what scope—micro or macro—do you evaluate?	☐ Component or course ☐ Specific courses ☐ Whole curriculum ☐ Particular company ☐ Particular industry ☐ Society as a whole	
Economic Role What are your economic roles in e-learning?	**Producer** ☐ Designer ☐ Builder ☐ Seller ☐ Distributor **Consumer** ☐ Purchaser ☐ Learner	
Timing When do you conduct evaluations?	☐ Before training is developed ☐ For an existing training package ☐ After training has been conducted	
Internal Versus External What characteristics do you evaluate?	☐ Internal development and management processes ☐ External results experienced by customers	
Levels What levels of outcomes do you evaluate?	☐ Level 1: Response ☐ Level 2: Learning ☐ Level 3: Performance ☐ Level 4: Business results	

3

Level 1: Response Evaluations

A level 1 evaluation measures the learner's response to training. Also referred to as a reaction or popularity evaluation, this level gauges the degree to which learners were satisfied with the way the training was conducted.

WHAT A RESPONSE EVALUATION TELLS YOU

A level 1, or response, evaluation reveals learners' immediate reaction to training. It can help answer questions such as these:

- Did training meet the expectations of learners?
- Did learners find the learning experience emotionally and intellectually satisfying?
- Did learners believe that they personally benefited from the training?
- Was the style of presentation (facilitator, displays, activities) acceptable to learners?
- How motivated were learners relative to the difficulties posed by the training?
- Did learners complete enough of the course for learning to take place?

Just as important as what a level 1 evaluation measures is what it *does not* measure. Several studies have found that whether learners liked a course correlated poorly with how much they learned or how well they were able to apply their learning (Dixon, 1990). In other words, level 1 evaluations do not measure training effectiveness.

REASONS TO PERFORM A LEVEL 1 EVALUATION

Level 1 evaluations can help you market and promote e-learning. For something as new as e-learning, overcoming initial widespread suspicions and doubts must be a high priority. Unless you can identify and correct problems that create negative feelings about e-learning, few learners will complete enough e-learning to accomplish anything productive.

Other uses for Level 1 evaluations include

- gauging whether learners feel comfortable and confident in their ability to take the course
- improving the style of the course and its presentation
- comparing the appeal of similar courses
- identifying unmotivated learners and the parts of the course that require more motivation than learners possess
- recognizing and defusing potential frustrations for learners
- developing your evaluation skills with the simplest form of evaluation.

TECHNIQUES FOR MEASURING RESPONSE

In conventional training, you gauge the response of learners in many different ways. Instructors take attendance by calling the roll or counting empty seats. Administrators calculate registration fees minus withdrawals. Comments from learners may be collected on Likert-scale questionnaires ("bingo cards") passed out at the end of the class. Additional comments may come from a posttraining focus group or exit interviews of individuals. Solicited and unsolicited testimonials, complaints, and suggestions provide additional feedback.

Level 1 evaluations for e-learning can use automated versions of many of the same techniques used in conventional training. Several additional techniques are also possible only in an electronic medium.

Electronically Track Access and Navigation

Web servers, collaboration software, and instructional management systems can log the actions of learners as they interact with the course. Such records can reveal the reactions of learners to individual pages and other components of the course. Reaction can be inferred from measures such as these:

- rate of progress through the course
- completion rates for individual lessons and activities
- assignments submitted
- number of pages accessed per day or week
- time when modules are accessed (day or night, workday or weekend)
- participation in online discussions and chat.

In analyzing access and activity logs, look for patterns and exceptions. For example, if the rate at which pages are accessed suddenly slows halfway through a certain lesson, you may have pinpointed a problem.

Do not confuse access and completion. Viewing a screen is not the same as completing a module. Skipped content may indicate that learners did not seriously attempt to learn or that they already knew the material in the skipped modules.

Administer Online Questionnaires

Use online forms to gather opinions from many learners. Make your questions clear, neutral, specific, and personal so they accurately record the opinion of an individual. Use questions such as those in figure 3-1 to assess the learner's response to a course.

Accept Feedback Within the Course

Because learners are already in the course, what better place to accept feedback from them? Comments entered into on-screen forms can be automatically collected, stored in a database, and summarized in reports (figure 3-2).

Figure 3-1. Example of an online questionnaire for a level 1 evaluation.

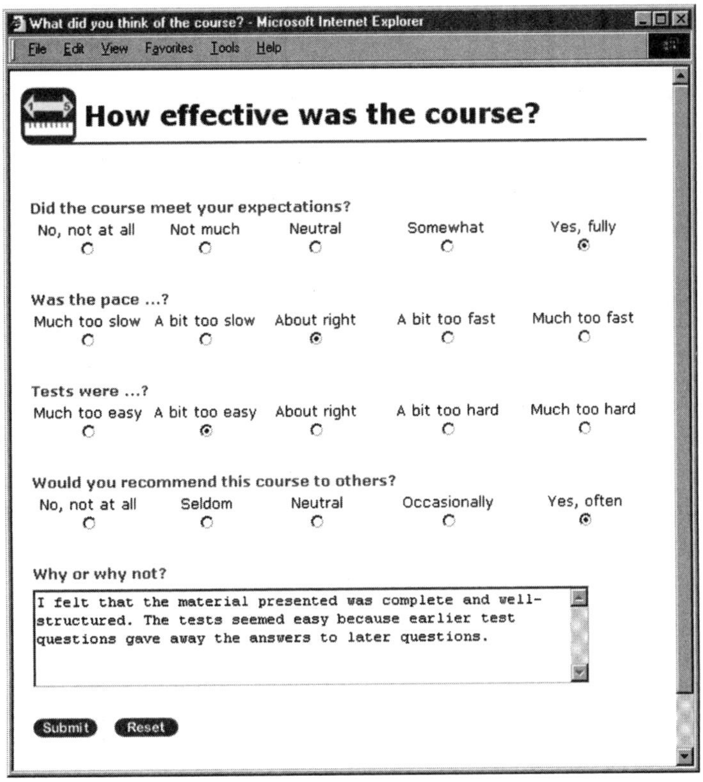

Figure 3-2. Example of an onscreen feedback form.

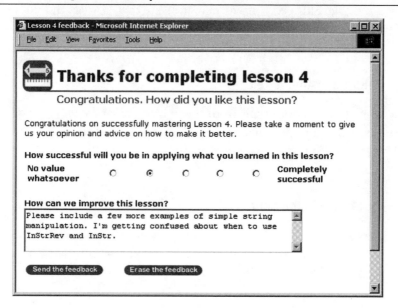

Because on-screen forms can be easier to fill in, completion rates may be higher and responses fuller. However, only those who go online will reach the form. Until participation is high, gather feedback by conventional means, too.

Let Learners Vote on Course Design

Voting inspires thought on the issues and encourages voters to take responsibility for their opinions. Voting also reveals the aggregate opinions of others. Figure 3-3 offers an example of learners voting on course design.

Virtual voting booths can let learners share their opinions on aspects of course design, making summaries immediately visible to all participants.

Discuss the Course With Learners

In a discussion forum, set up a discussion thread for learners to express their reaction to various aspects of the course. Online discussions allow learners to see and probe the opinions of others. Figure 3-4 is an example of an online discussion on course design. To provoke fruitful debate, seed the discussion with statements about the course and challenge learners to agree or disagree with the statement.

Hold Online Focus Groups

If chat or instant messaging is a part of the course and participants are fluent typists in a common language, consider conducting an online focus group, such as the one depicted in figure 3-5.

Figure 3-3. Example of an e-learning "ballot."

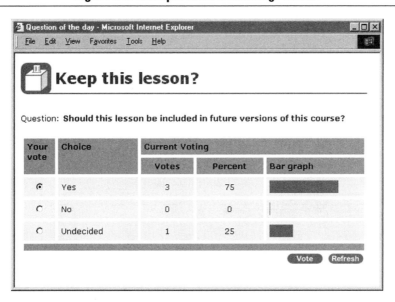

Such an online chat session has the advantage that the moderator does not have to frantically jot down notes during the session or laboriously transcribe an audio recording afterwards.

Figure 3-4. Example of an online discussion forum for evaluating an e-learning course.

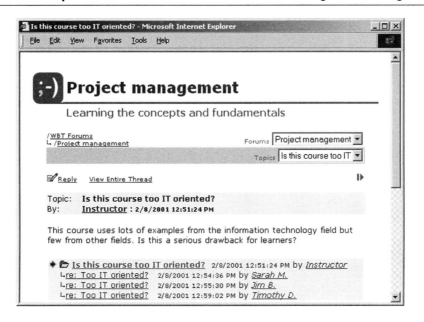

Figure 3-5. Example of an online focus group.

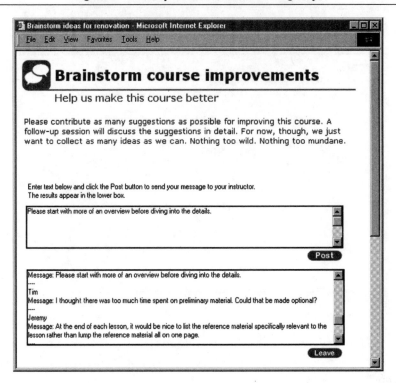

Let Learners Express Feelings

Let learners express a range of feelings beyond simple approval and disapproval. Ask learners how they feel about an issue, rather than merely whether they agree or disagree with a statement (figure 3-6).

Invite Comments and Suggestions Anytime

Good evaluation requires attentive listening. Do not make learners wait until the end of a lesson to voice their opinions. Invite them to offer comments and suggestions at any point. Provide a button on each page of the course to trigger a short, pre-addressed, online feedback form, such as the one shown in figure 3-7.

TIPS FOR MEASURING

Here are some simple ways you can improve the level 1 evaluation process and its results:

■ *Consider the novelty of e-learning.* E-learning is new. Learners may find it strange and unfamiliar. Their responses may not accurately predict the long-term potential of your efforts. Before evaluating e-learning,

Figure 3-6. How to elicit learners' feelings.

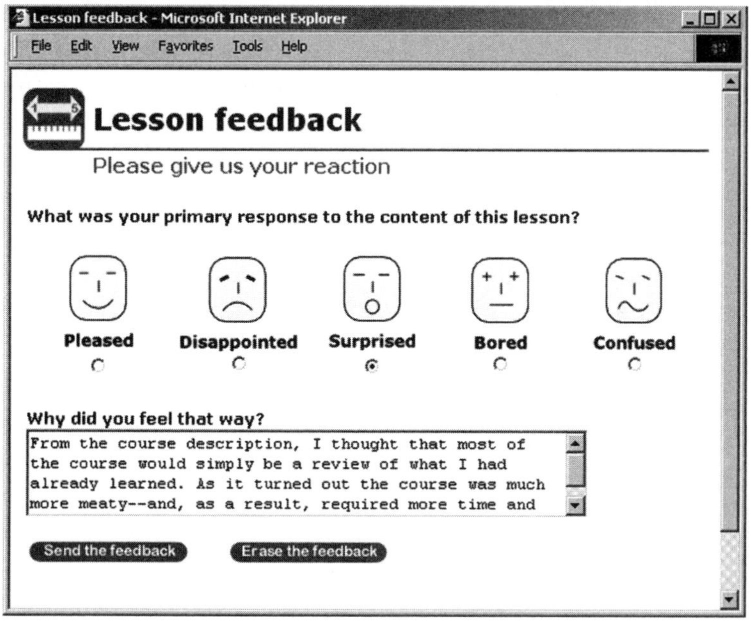

Figure 3-7. Example of an online feedback form that learners can access from every page.

Why High Dropout Rates Aren't Necessarily Bad

Ahigh dropout rate means your e-learning is not working, right? After all, you would not sanction a classroom course if 80 percent of the students stood up and walked out after a few hours.

For a medium as new as e-learning, you may want to delay judgment until you fully understand what the high dropout rates really indicate. Perhaps learners were just taste-testing e-learning. Some probably thought that e-learning would not require hard work on their part. You should also realize that many learners stay in classroom training only because of social and organizational pressure to remain. Dropping out of classroom training can incur considerable embarrassment. Dropping out of e-learning requires only an anonymous mouse click.

Dropout may just indicate an empowered learner exercising good time management skills. Many quit because they learned all they needed to.

make sure that all learners surveyed have the basic e-learning and computer skills necessary to benefit from the course. And, expect a high dropout rate for early courses.

■ *Analyze data to gain insights.* Use response data to pinpoint problem areas in your courses. Monitor when and where learners give up. Try to figure out why learners quit.

■ *Do not wait till the end of the course.* Get feedback frequently. Level 1 evaluations are most often performed at the end of the course. However, results may be more informative if they are performed throughout the course for individual lessons or topics. Such piecemeal evaluations are especially useful because they can capture opinions of learners who become embittered or drop out before completing the course.

YOUR TURN

Level 1 evaluations measure the immediate response of learners to training. Such evaluations help you better target and market e-learning.

What can a response evaluation tell you? Why might your organization conduct a level 1 evaluation of its e-learning? On worksheet 3-1, list specific questions such an evaluation could answer.

Worksheet 3-1. Choosing the right question to get the right information.	
Response Question You Will Ask	**What the Response Can Tell You**

You will likely be able to draw upon your repertoire of techniques that you already use for evaluating conventional training. Which of these techniques will you use to evaluate e-learning? Try worksheet 3-2.

Worksheet 3-2. Apply your proven evaluation methods to e-learning.		
Level 1 Evaluation Technique	**Used for Conventional Training (Yes/No)**	**Will Use for E-Learning? (Yes/No)**
Questionnaires		
Feedback within the course		
Learners voting on course design		
Discussions with learners		
Focus groups		
Comments outside the course		
Other:		
Other:		
Other:		

Now it is time to move beyond the methods you use for evaluating conventional training. E-learning opens the door to a whole new realm of evaluation methods because it exists in an electronic, automated environment. Which electronic techniques will you use to conduct level 1 evaluations of e-learning? Use worksheet 3-3 to answer this question.

Worksheet 3-3. Identify ways to use automated evaluation methods for level 1 evaluation.

Electronic Technique	Suitable for E-Learning? (Yes/No)	How Will You Use This Technique?
Track access and navigation		
Online surveys and questionnaires		
Email address for feedback		
Onscreen feedback forms		
Discussion forum for course quality		
Online focus groups		
Other:		
Other:		
Other:		

4

Level 2:
Level 2:
Learning Evaluations

L evel 2, or learning, evaluations measure what the student learned. Sometimes called knowledge evaluations, Level 2 evaluations measure whether the original learning objectives of the course were met. Level 2 evaluations help you identify the specific facts, concepts, skills, attitudes, and beliefs learners acquired in training. They can also help you see to what degree course content, presentation, and structure support learning.

REASONS TO PERFORM A LEVEL 2 EVALUATION

Use a level 2 evaluation to see how much learners actually learn. A level 2 evaluation is especially effective in finding ways to improve the amount of knowledge transferred. Use a level 2 evaluation when:

- Job performance depends directly on the specific knowledge learned. Thus, a learning evaluation predicts improvements in job performance.
- You are teaching generic skills and knowledge that may be applied in many different kinds of jobs so that higher-level evaluations are not practical.
- A meaningful yet economical evaluation is required. Much of the level 2 evaluation can be automated.

HOW TO MEASURE LEARNING

An effective level 2 evaluation examines the right units at the right time. Learning, at least for evaluation purposes, is most commonly measured at the end of the training course. Though logical, this timing may not yield the most complete or meaningful results. By measuring at the beginning and during the course, you can pinpoint the effectiveness of specific topics and activities within. Such information is vital in refining the course content and presentation.

Measuring knowledge only at the end of the course can be misleading. Many studies have found that without reinforcement, knowledge levels may drop precipitously after training (Baddeley, 1990). Up to 80 to 90 percent of the knowledge measured at the end of a training class may be lost within a few weeks. A more effective measurement of actual learning can be made after knowledge levels reach equilibrium, say six weeks after training.

For external evaluations aimed at demonstrating the value of e-learning, you probably want to evaluate entire courses. For internal evaluations seeking to improve course design, you will want to evaluate the effectiveness of smaller units, such as individual lessons or even topics and activities.

TECHNIQUES FOR MEASURING LEARNING

Learning has conventionally been measured both by tests and by the opinions of teachers. E-learning can build on these techniques.

Conventional training has used either final examinations to measure absolute knowledge levels or a combination of pre- and posttests to measure improvements in the levels of knowledge. Conventional training also relies on independent, standardized certification, licensure, or accreditation tests. These include those administered by government licensing boards and industry organizations as well as those by specific companies, such as Microsoft, Cisco, and Novell, to measure knowledge of their particular technologies.

A more subjective measure of learning may come from the opinions of trainers, facilitators, and teaching assistants who have observed the behavior of learners in the classroom. Such opinions are guided by questions asked and answered by students and their participation in team activities. E-learning can use automated versions of these conventional techniques as well as additional electronic techniques.

Design Tests to Evaluate Learning

Much has been written about testing to measure individual learners. Table 4-1 and the companion Website (www.horton.com/evaluating/) offer some pointers along these lines. The aggregate results of such tests can provide an effective evaluation of the course itself.

In using tests to evaluate e-learning, it is important to keep in mind the subtle differences between helping individuals learn effectively and helping organizations evaluate the effectiveness of training programs. Sometimes your goals may be at odds with one another. Time limits, for example, may

Table 4-1. Write test questions to measure knowledge.

Question Format	When to Use This Question Format	Tips for Using This Question Format
True/False Learner picks one of two mutually exclusive choices.	• To test the learner's ability to make categorical judgments and to pick between true opposites • To simulate job activities that require yes/no, go/no-go, approve/disapprove, or pass/fail kinds of decisions	• Ask more questions to eliminate guessing. • Phrase the question in neutral terms so as not to give away the answer. • Phrase questions in various ways so the right answer is sometimes true and sometimes false.
Pick One Learner picks one item from a list of choices.	• For activities that require learners to assign items to well-defined categories • For questions with one right answer	• Include at least four plausible alternatives. • Require thought, not process of elimination, to answer questions. • Include nearly right and barely wrong answers to sharpen the test.
Pick Multiple Learner can choose multiple items from a list.	• For more sophisticated questions with more than one right answer	• Include nearly right and barely wrong answers to sharpen the test.
Text Input Learner answers in a free-form, essay style.	• To verify knowledge of names, numbers, and other textual information • For free-form, essay style questions, assuming that human scoring is possible	• Phrase the question to limit the number and form of correct answers. • Accept synonyms, grammatical variants, and some misspellings. • Ask only one simple question per input box.
Fill-in-the-Blank Learner is required to provide a short answer.	• To test detailed knowledge, such as terminology, language syntax, or mathematical formulas • To provide some "scaffolding," or context, for learners	• Make the context realistic. • Fully introduce the scenario or context. • Use selection lists if spelling is not critical or there are too many right answers.
Matching Lists Learner matches items from one list to corresponding items in another list.	• To measure knowledge of the relationship among concepts or objects, like tools and their uses, terms and their definitions, etc.	• Keep the lists short so that both fit in the same display. • Do not make learners type answers. • Use selection lists or drag-and-drop symbols to indicate matches. • Include at least one "no-match" item.
Click-in Picture Learner answers by pointing to an object or area in a picture.	• To test visual recognition of an object, area, or subsystem	• Make click targets visually distinct. • Make click targets large enough—at least 20 × 20 pixels. • Show the scene, as it would appear in the real world.

discourage learners from thinking about what they are doing or experimenting to find better solutions. In such cases, tests with time limits may reduce the effectiveness of learning. On the other hand, monitoring the time required by learners to perform actions may provide a valuable indicator of the quality and depth of learning.

Likewise, tracking the number of tries may discourage learners from exploring and experimenting on their own, thereby denying them the benefit of feedback received as a result of making "wrong" choices. Yet, the number of wrong steps indicates depth of learning. One possible compromise is to track time and tries for purposes of evaluating the course but not to use these measurements for scoring individual learners.

Observe Learners' Behavior During Training

E-learning provides opportunities to monitor learners by observing the behavior of participants in learning activities. Course facilitators can look at discussion groups and chat transcripts for evidence of learning, performance improvement, or attitude shift. To reveal deeper learning, challenge learners to summarize discussions and to post original questions for others to answer. To reduce the subjective nature of such observations, define a procedure and formula for conducting such observations and scoring the results.

Challenge Learners to Perform Live, Hands-on Activities

To measure the ability to perform manual tasks, you can simply have learners perform them. For live, hands-on activities, give learners a well-defined task to perform. The example in figure 4-1 requires learners to use the system calculator to convert numbers from decimal form to hexadecimal and octal equivalents. (You can jump to this example from this book's companion Website at www.horton.com/evaluating/.)

In hands-on activities, monitor performance with a series of "gatekeeper" questions. To answer each gatekeeper question, learners must have performed the preceding step in the procedure. In this example, the question asks about menus revealed only by successful completion of the required step in the procedure. For finer discrimination, you can track the timing of completion for these gatekeeper activities.

Another approach, often used in combination with the first, is to give a sample of real-world tasks to perform. This approach is depicted in figure 4-2 in which the learner is asked to convert a series of numbers from one form to another.

Hands-on activities are valuable when measuring the ability to operate a computer program or piece of equipment.

Figure 4-1. Example of a hands-on learning activity.

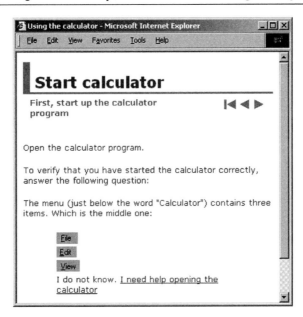

Simulate Actual Work Activities

Use online simulations to test performance of complex activities, especially ones too expensive or dangerous to perform for real. Such simulations measure whether the learner can apply knowledge and skills in a realistic setting. They are also useful for evaluating any knowledge best learned by doing.

Figure 4-2. Example of using gatekeeper questions to monitor e-learners' progress.

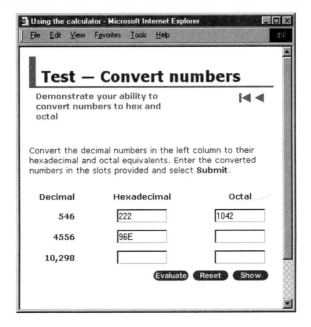

The example in figure 4-3 shows a simulation used to test the learner's ability to create a database connection. (You can link to this example from this book's companion Website at www.horton.com/evaluating/.) A simulation was necessary because the procedure is complex and, if done incorrectly, could damage the learner's system.

If you use simulations, be sure they require authentic skills and decision making. Fully explain the simulation and its goals—and make clear its limitations. Do not give learners more choices or options than necessary for a realistic measurement of knowledge or skills.

Conduct Role-Playing Activities

Online role-playing activities provide an opportunity to evaluate how well a group of learners can perform complex, interpersonal tasks. Learners are presented with a scenario and are assigned roles to play. Each learner is given a separate identity with specific goals, knowledge, and biases. For example, in a class on architectural design for remodeling contractors, learners may be assigned the task of simulating a meeting of the architectural review committee (see figure 4-4).

Figure 4-3. Example of how simulation can be used to evaluate e-learning.

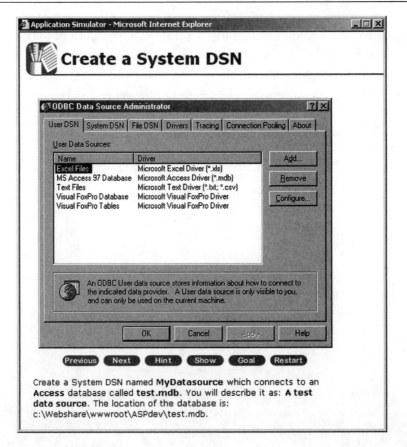

**Figure 4-4. Example of a role-playing activity
for assessing learners' abilities to handle complex tasks.**

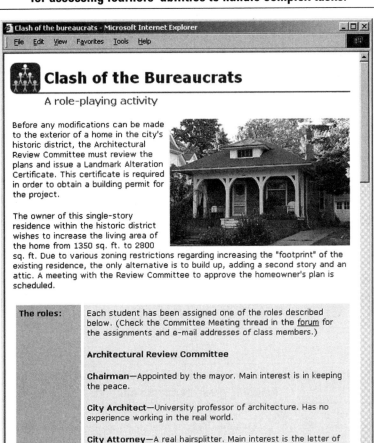

Meetings, held in chat sessions or a discussion forum, can provide evidence of learning and ability (figure 4-5).

Role-playing scenarios allow realistic interaction without requiring everyone to be at the same place. They are good for all forms of training that involve complex human activities, especially ones dependent on interpersonal relationships. Use them to evaluate teamwork and organizational dynamics, ability to see things from the viewpoint of others, willingness to compromise and accommodate, and ability to lead and motivate others.

Survey Those Who Should Know

Survey questionnaires are not the best way to measure learning, given the more direct methods of testing and observing performance. However, survey questionnaires can round out your understanding by gauging learners' confidence in what they have learned. Figure 4-6 lists some kinds of survey questions that can be used to measure learning effectiveness.

Figure 4-5. Use discussion forums to evaluate e-learners' progress in role-playing activities.

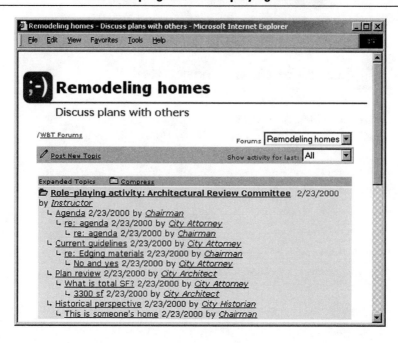

Figure 4-6. Examples of some survey questions that can gauge learners' grasp of course content.

How will you do your job differently as a result of the training you have received?

> I will be more willing to point out the advantages of our high-margin products to potential customers because I feel more confident in my understanding of them.

How confident are you that you can meet each of these course objectives?

Objective	Confidence
Recall the three main advantages of each of the high-margin products.	98 %
Identify the customer benefits resulting from each product advantage.	90 %
For individual customers, cite three reasons to purchase a high-margin product.	95 %

For each individual customer, how well could you identify the benefits of high-margin products?

Before training:

Not at all ○ 1 ● 2 ○ 3 ○ 4 ○ 5 Fully

After training:

Not at all ○ 1 ○ 2 ○ 3 ○ 4 ● 5 Fully

Play Learning Games

Learning games are simulations styled as play. They can be just as rigorous and realistic as conventional simulations. Like regular simulations, learning games can evaluate the acquisition of complex skills and knowledge that cannot be reduced to a list of facts or step-by-step procedures or that must be applied in unpredictable circumstances.

In the tree farming game (figure 4-7), players learn to manage a pine forest in the southeastern United States. (You can link to this example from this book's companion Website at www.horton.com/evaluating/.)

Learners can be challenged to meet specific timber management goals, such as making the most money in the shortest time, leaving their heirs the most valuable property possible, improving environmental conditions, or achieving some combination of these goals. In forestry, growth cycles are measured in

Figure 4-7. Games can be used to evaluate complex knowledge and skills.

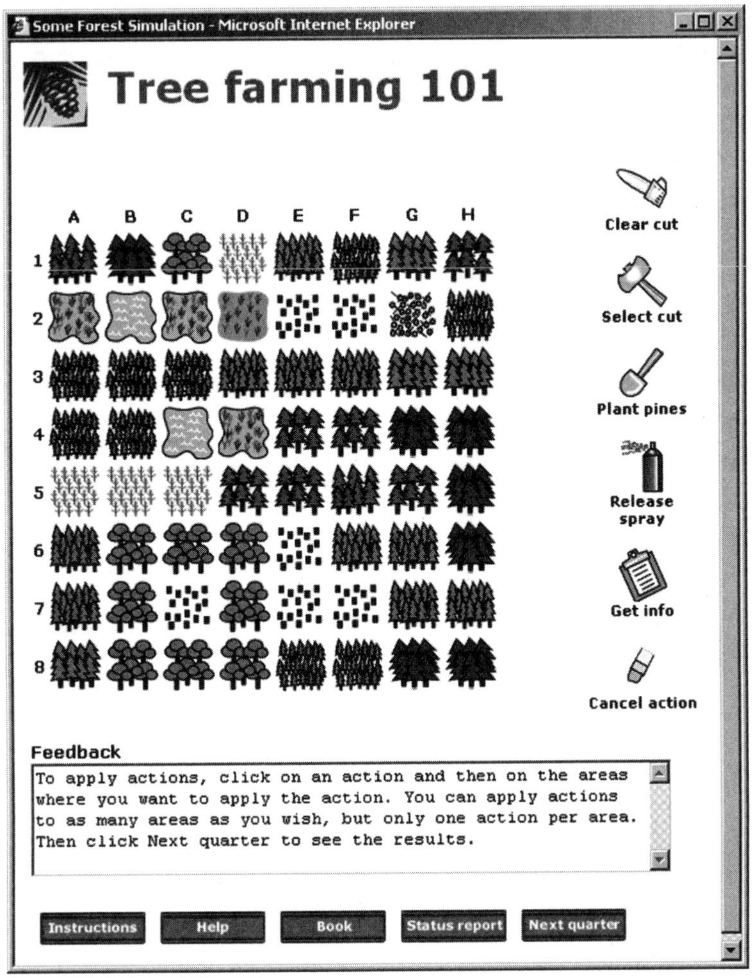

31

decades and subject to unpredictable factors such as weather, fluctuating prices, and insect infestation. Learners may spend hours or days playing and replaying such a game. In a well-designed learning game, winning the game demonstrates accomplishment of specific learning objectives. Monitor aspects of the game that most clearly indicate successful learning.

Your Turn

Level 2 evaluations measure how much students learned, typically by testing them or observing their behavior. Learning evaluations are common in classroom training, and, armed with this book, you should have no trouble extending conventional techniques to work for evaluating e-learning. First, consider the techniques you use to measure accomplishment of learning objectives in your conventional classroom training (worksheet 4-1). Which of these techniques can you use, with appropriate modifications, in e-learning?

Worksheet 4-1. How do you evaluate learning today?		
Level 2 Evaluation Technique	**Used in Conventional Training (Yes/No)**	**Will Use in E-Learning? (Yes/No)**
Tests and examinations		
Observing learners' behavior		
Hands-on activities		
Simulated work activities		
Role-playing activities		
Surveys of persons who can rate learning		
Learning games		

Next review table 4-1 and determine what kind of test questions will best evaluate learners' gains in skills and knowledge in your e-learning courses. Complete worksheet 4-2 to help you develop appropriate test questions.

Besides tests, what other evaluation techniques will you use to measure the learning produced by e-learning in your organization? With worksheet 4-3, consider some of the exciting possibilities available in the e-world.

Worksheet 4-2. What kinds of test questions will you use to measure learning from your e-learning courses?

Question Format	What These Kinds of Questions Will Measure
True/False	
Pick one	
Pick multiple	
Text input (free-form, essay style)	
Fill-in-the-blanks	
Matching lists	
Click-in picture	

Worksheet 4-3. What other level 2 evaluation techniques will you use?

Technique	What It Will Measure	How Will You Use It?
Observing learners' behavior		
Hands-on activities		
Simulated work activities		
Role-playing activities		
Surveys of persons who can rate learning		
Learning games		

5

Level 3: Performance Evaluations

Level 3 evaluations measure job performance. This level, sometimes called application, measures to what degree learners can and do apply learning in the context of their jobs. A level 3 evaluation answers questions such as these:

- How much better can learners perform their jobs as a result of training?
- Do trainees apply what they learned at the right time and in an appropriate, accurate way?
- What specific skills, knowledge, and attitudes were transferred to the workplace?

REASONS TO CONDUCT A LEVEL 3 EVALUATION

A performance evaluation is called for when the gap between knowing and doing is critical to business success. Use a level 3 evaluation where training is targeted at directly improving on-the-job (OJT) performance. Though costly, level 3 evaluations are worthwhile if failure to apply knowledge and skills has been a problem or if putting theory into practice is a high priority within the organization.

Use a level 3 evaluation to identify factors that limit how well learners apply learning. A successful level 3 evaluation can identify factors such as the following:

- Are learners motivated to improve performance?
- Do they believe what they learned really applies to their jobs?
- Can they spot events that should trigger application of learning?
- Can learners recall specific procedures, facts, and principles in the context of the work environment?

Level 3 evaluations help you target job-critical skills and remove barriers to applying learning on the job.

How to Measure Performance

Because performance occurs outside the e-learning environment, evaluation may be outside too—though some techniques may have an electronic twist. As with other levels of evaluation, success requires measuring the right units at the right time. Measure performance for the entire course or for individual performance objectives within it. Measuring smaller units may not yield meaningful results and may prove too expensive to perform.

Give training time to take hold. Test and measure job performance after application levels stabilize, usually 30 to 180 days after training. Allow enough time for workers to become comfortable applying learning and for adequate opportunities to apply learning to accumulate. If opportunities for applying knowledge are infrequent, you must measure over a period long enough for a meaningful number of occurrences.

Integrate Performance Evaluation With Other Performance Efforts

Measuring performance is an integral part of the management function of any large organization. Ally your efforts to evaluate the effects of e-learning with other corporate efforts such as enterprise resource planning, HR administration, competency development models, succession planning, and career development planning.

Techniques for Measuring Performance

Fortunately, techniques for measuring and observing job performance are well established and highly refined. The electronic environment of e-learning automates and streamlines this process.

Observe Behavior on the Job

To measure on-the-job performance, observe attempts to apply learning to realistic situations. Provide a checklist for scoring the learner's behavior in a simulated or real application of learning. For example, a sales training course might include a list for scoring a sales interview (figure 5-1).

Gather Opinions of Those Who Should Know

You can gauge performance, especially of interpersonal skills, by collecting the informed opinions of those in positions to observe the behavior of trainees on the job. You can use online and conventional means to conduct survey questionnaires, interviews, or focus groups to gather information from supervisors, peers, subordinates, and the trainees themselves.

Figure 5-1. Evaluating sales training on the job.

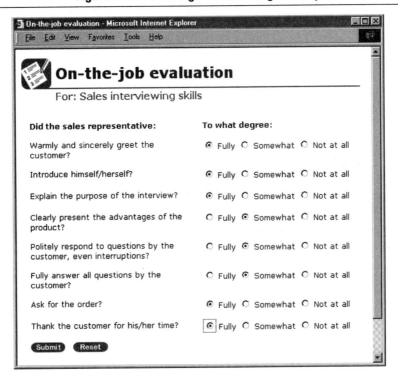

Ask specific questions that reveal how much performance has improved and what portion of that improvement is due to training. Figure 5-2 lists some sample questions you can use to gather such evaluations.

Consult Job Performance Records

You can save considerable time and expense if performance can be deduced or inferred from job performance records routinely collected by the organization. What kinds of measurements can you use to measure the results of training? Consider the following sources:

- *sales records:* sales volume, new customers, customer retention, new inquiries, repeat orders
- *quality records:* number of defects, returned goods, product recalls, number of complaints, required maintenance and repairs
- *service records:* number of customers handled, time customers spend waiting, customer satisfaction ratings, number of customer complaints
- *safety records:* number of accidents, time between accidents, insurance claims, insurance rates

Figure 5-2. Examples of questions for eliciting feedback about the learner's performance improvement.

What are you, your supervisor, peers, subordinates doing to apply <*subject of training*>?

How did what you learned in <*training course*> help you on your job?

To what extent did you apply <*skill or technique*> during your most recent <*activity presenting an opportunity to apply training*>?

Not at all ○ 1 ○ 2 ◉ 3 ○ 4 ○ 5 Fully

Estimate the time you have saved due to <*learning objective*>: ☐ hours/week

In what percentage of <*opportunities to apply learning*> did you apply what you learned?

Before training: ☐ %
After training: ☐ %

To what extent has <*course name*> improved your performance on the job? ☐ %

Before the course, how often did <*event or behavior*> occur? Every ☐ days

Now how often does <*event or behavior*> occur? Every ☐ days

- *productivity records:* deadlines met and missed, downtime, output per person or machine
- *employment records:* employee satisfaction records, turnover, absenteeism, open positions, labor grievances, lawsuits.

Test Performance With a Control Group

A more scientific (and expensive) approach is to compare the performance of a group that receives training to that of an identical group that does not (figure 5-3). For this approach, you must recruit test participants and randomly assign them to two groups. One group receives training and the other (the control group) does not. Then, compare the work performance of the two groups. The difference represents the improvement due to training.

Figure 5-3. Using experimental and control groups to evaluate e-learning.

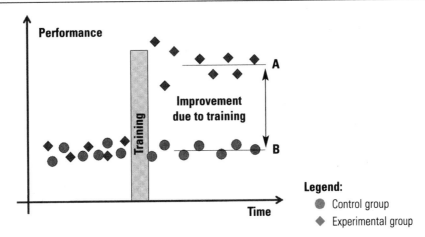

Remember: Do not measure performance immediately after training. Allow enough time (usually 30 to 180 days) for learners to become accustomed to applying what they learned on the job.

Analyze Performance Trends

Testing with a control group has two drawbacks. First, it requires many test subjects, and, second, it does not account for ongoing changes in job performance due to other factors. Over the period of the test, the president of the

---

S...s...s...statistics?

If your comparisons of performance are to have meaning and to carry weight with management, tests should follow good statistical techniques of data gathering and analysis. You must make your decision of statistical technique before you begin collecting data, because the technique you choose will determine such things as the number of test subjects
needed, the accuracy to which data must be measured, and how you handle exceptional cases, such as learners who quit the company in the middle of the test.

If you are not an expert in statistics, don't panic. The kinds of comparisons you are doing do not require the same degree of scientific rigor as demanded of medical and scientific research. You can pick up much of what you need from a couple of good books on statistical measurement techniques. You could start with lighthearted *The Cartoon Guide to Statistics* by Larry Gonick and Woollcott Smith and progress to the complete and authoritative *Statistics for Experimenters: An Introduction to Design, Data Analysis, and Model Building* by George E.P. Box.

If you are still not comfortable defining your statistical procedures, consider hiring a consultant to design the experiment for you and train you to conduct it and to analyze your data.

company may deliver an inspirational speech to employees, a sudden souring of the stock market may render stock options less valuable, or a competitor may announce a superior product. Anything that affects morale affects performance. Also over the training period, workers continue to gain more experience in their jobs just by doing it. Because all of these factors affect both the control and test groups, it is tempting to ignore them. But such factors could mean that performance would change regardless of whether training is conducted. We must be careful to isolate the changes due to training.

A slightly more sophisticated technique helps focus on the changes due to training by monitoring trends in the performance levels of a group before and after training. This technique is commonly called trend-line analysis (figure 5-4).

In this approach, you monitor performance of a single group before it receives training and again over a period of time after it receives training. It is important to monitor trends, not just levels, so that you can discount the effect of other interventions implicit in the baseline trends that may be active at the time of training. Again, it is important to allow enough time after training to establish the new trend.

Monitor Action Plans

Many organizations, as part of performance appraisal and improvement efforts, require employees to prepare action plans or performance contracts. Such plans document specific steps the employee and others will take to improve performance. Monitoring the fulfillment of such plans can provide direct evidence of the effects of learning.

Figure 5-4. Using trend-line analysis to evaluate e-learning.

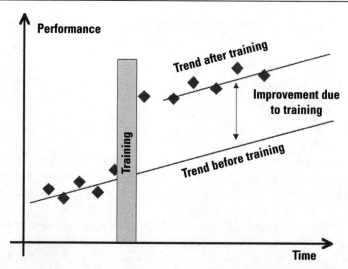

An action plan tracks the accomplishment of the performance objectives for an individual. An action plan may look something like figure 5-5.

The due date for each objective can trigger an email to the evaluator requesting a rating of how well the person responsible has accomplished the objective. Figures 5-6 and 5-7 show how this can be done.

Simulate Job Performance

Testing performance with computer simulations can help predict job performance. Such simulations reveal whether learners can apply knowledge and skills—but not whether they actually will. Still, simulations may provide a low-cost way of predicting job performance, especially for dangerous or difficult skills.

Figure 5-5. Action plan for evaluating target performance.

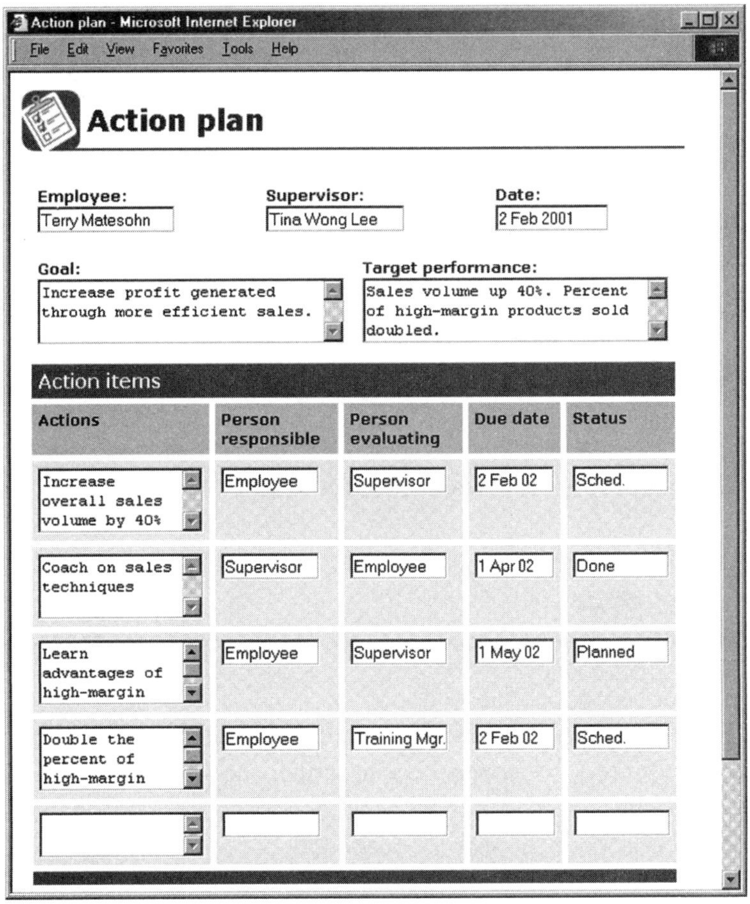

Figure 5-6. Example of an email you can send to trigger an evaluation.

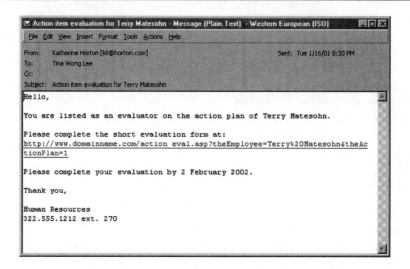

Figure 5-7. Clicking the link in the email brings up the evaluation form.

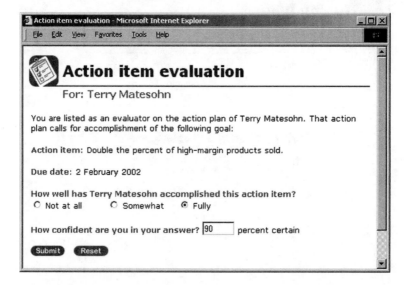

For simulations to accurately predict OTJ performance, they must realistically mimic the job environment in which the performance must occur. This means that the simulation must provide the same cues for action and the same distractions as the real work environment.

YOUR TURN

Unless training somehow improves job performance, it is of questionable value. Most organizations routinely measure job performance as part of their ongoing efforts to improve quality and productivity and as part of their employment appraisal efforts. Performance evaluations for training can draw on these existing measures and add ones tuned especially for e-learning.

How does your organization measure job performance now? Can any of the measurements listed on worksheet 5-1 be used to evaluate the effectiveness of training?

Worksheet 5-1. How do you measure performance now?		
Technique for Measuring Job Performance	**Used in Your Organization? (Yes/No)**	**Suitable for Evaluating Training? (Yes/No)**
Observing OTJ behavior		
Opinions of those who can rate worker's performance		
Job-performance records		
Controlled tests of work output		
Analysis of performance trends		
Monitoring action plans		
Simulations of work activities		
Other:		
Other:		
Other:		

Of the techniques listed in this chapter, which ones best meet your evaluation needs? How do they match your budget, schedule, learners, subject matter, and other constraints (worksheet 5-2)? Feel free to add more techniques that you plan to use to evaluate e-learning.

Worksheet 5-2. How will you measure e-learning performance?		
Technique for Measuring Job Performance	**Suitable for Evaluating Your E-Learning? (Yes/No)**	**How Will You Use It?**
Observing OTJ behavior		
Opinions of those who can rate worker's performance		
Job performance records		
Controlled tests of work output		
Analysis of performance trends		
Monitoring action plans		
Simulations of work activities		
Other:		
Other:		
Other:		

6

Level 4: Results Evaluations

Trainees loved your training, they learned everything you presented, and they are applying everything they learned. Yet management seems skeptical about funding additional programs. The costs of providing training were high, and questions remain about whether the organization is any better off because of your training. How can you demonstrate that training is indeed a good business investment?

A level 4 evaluation may be the answer. Level 4 evaluations measure the business results of learning. They help you answer such questions as these:

- Is training contributing directly to the business objectives of the organization?
- Did the training accomplish its original business and organizational goals?
- How much have essential business processes (quality, efficiency, and productivity) improved as a result of training?
- How does the rate of return on money invested in training compare to other investments open to the organization?

REASONS TO EVALUATE BUSINESS RESULTS

The business results of training are extremely difficult and expensive to measure precisely. Substantial business results take so long to achieve and depend on so many factors that attributing business results to a single training effort can prove time-consuming, difficult, and frustrating. No wonder that level 4 evaluations are seldom undertaken.

In some cases, however, the value of a level 4 evaluation can offset the difficulty and uncertainty of conducting such an evaluation. Consider a level 4 evaluation for these purposes:

■ *To align training efforts to the basic business goals of the organization:* A level 4 evaluation can demonstrate fiscal responsibility and attention to organizational priorities.

■ *To decide among various solutions to a tough business problem:* Use a level 4 evaluation to compare training to other business solutions or to pick among several training solutions.

■ *To document the benefits of training:* A level 4 evaluation may be just the ticket to demonstrate the business value of e-learning to tightfisted business executives or skeptical customers.

How to Measure Business Results

To measure business results, you must carefully define the results you will monitor and precisely document the effect of training on those results. Calculating business results for a single course may be impossible because the effect of a single course may be insignificant or intermingled with the effects of many other causes. A better approach may be to measure the effect of an entire curriculum or training program.

Business results, especially those of broad significance, take time to accrue. When evaluating the effects of e-learning, you must ask yourself how long to wait before results will be apparent. And, you must ask over how long a period you should monitor such results. It is not unusual to wait 12 months after training to monitor results and to measure results over a six-month period.

When measuring business results, it is important to not overstate the contribution of training. You should ask how much of the results are due to training and how sure you are of that estimate. Figure 6-1 shows an example of a questionnaire completed by a sales manager.

By multiplying the value of the change ($15,000) by the percentage due to training (55 percent) and by the confidence rating (75 percent), you arrive at a confident, but conservative, estimate of the financial value of training. From the figures in figure 6-1, the sales manager confidently claims that training yielded benefits over $6,000 per month.

Techniques for Measuring Results

Measuring the business results of training is essentially no different from measuring business results from any other kind of effort. You must identify indicators of success and track how they are influenced by training.

Figure 6-1. Example of a questionnaire completed by a sales manager.

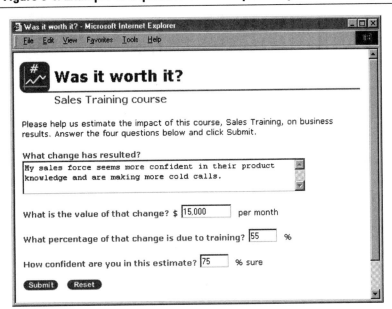

Calculate Return-on-Investment (ROI)

The most commonly used measure of business success is ROI. It measures the financial rewards of an initial outlay. The basic formula for ROI is simple: ROI equals return divided by investment. Let's say you invest $100,000 in a project. The results of the project are a $20,000 per year increase in revenue or savings. You would say that this project has a ROI of $20,000 divided by $100,000 or 20 percent. Though simple, ROI is a very flexible measure of business success. You can adapt it to specific purposes by what you choose to measure as return, investment, and time frame.

For example, to a training supplier, investment might represent the costs of developing and offering courses. Return could come from sales and licensing fees for the course. For an organization buying training from an outside supplier, the investment is the cost of licensing or purchasing the e-learning products. The return comes from improved job performance by employees of the organization.

You could use ROI to decide whether to convert internal training from the classroom to e-learning. In this case, the investment would be the cost of developing or purchasing equally effective e-learning. The returns would be the savings in travel, instructor salaries, and other costs of conducting classroom training. More details on how to calculate ROI for e-learning are found in chapter 7.

Calculate Other Financial Measures

Most organizations state the projected value of a project in terms of ROI. There are, however, other ways of stating the same results. If your management prefers a different formula, use that formula. Here are some different approaches:

- *Benefit-cost ratio:* Some organizations express gain as a ratio of benefits to costs. Say, for example, your project yields benefits of $150,000 and costs $100,000. Its benefit-cost ratio would be $150,000/$100,000, or 1.5.
- *Net present value:* This measure is more commonly used during periods of high interest rates and inflation and is still used on multiyear projects. It calculates total benefits throughout the span of the project and then discounts these benefits to present dollars using an assumed interest rate or required rate of return. For example, if a project costs $100,000 up front but yields a return of $30,000 per year for five years, its net present value, assuming an 8 percent interest rate, would be $29,364.
- *Time to payback:* How long must an organization wait for the benefits to equal the initial investment? This period of time is referred to as time to payback. For example, if a project requires an up-front investment of $100,000 and returns $10,000 per month, its time to payback is 10 months.
- *Learners to payback:* For training projects, managers often want to know how many learners they must train to recover the costs of developing and offering training. Suppose training requires $100,000 to develop and $100 per person to offer. Each person trained yields a benefit of $300, for a net benefit of $200 per learner trained. At that rate, development costs are repaid by training 500 people, which equals the initial $100,000 invested divided by the savings of $200 per learner trained.

Monitor Business Metrics

You can save considerable time and effort by basing your evaluation on currently collected measures of business success. If such measures accurately reflect the business goals you are trying to accomplish, changes in these measures will provide clear evidence of the effectiveness of training.

Metrics of business success that your organization may be collecting now include these:

- profitability (revenue, profit, profit margin)
- financial health (stock price, cash reserves, market share, inventory levels)

- customers (accounts, clients, sponsors)
- intellectual capital (education level of staff or new hires; professional experience of staff or new hires; proportion of professional, administrative, and manufacturing staff)
- reputation (industry awards, rankings, ratings).

Consider Nonmonetary Measures of Business Success

In many cases, nonmonetary returns may be larger and more important than the monetary ones. In some organizations, especially during early phases of their development, goals other than immediate financial success predominate. Such goals include reducing the time required to bring a product to market, achieving technical superiority in a particular market, and enhancing the prestige of the organization. Documenting e-learning's contribution toward achieving these goals may do more for getting your project approved than a high ROI figure.

Always consider the contribution of training to themes valuable to management. To detect these themes, read executive statements in annual reports, scan the walls for posters, and look at internal memos and email. Also, consider the value of e-learning in portraying an image of the training department as forward thinking, technically innovative, and financially adept.

Figure 6-2. Use survey instruments to estimate business results of e-learning.

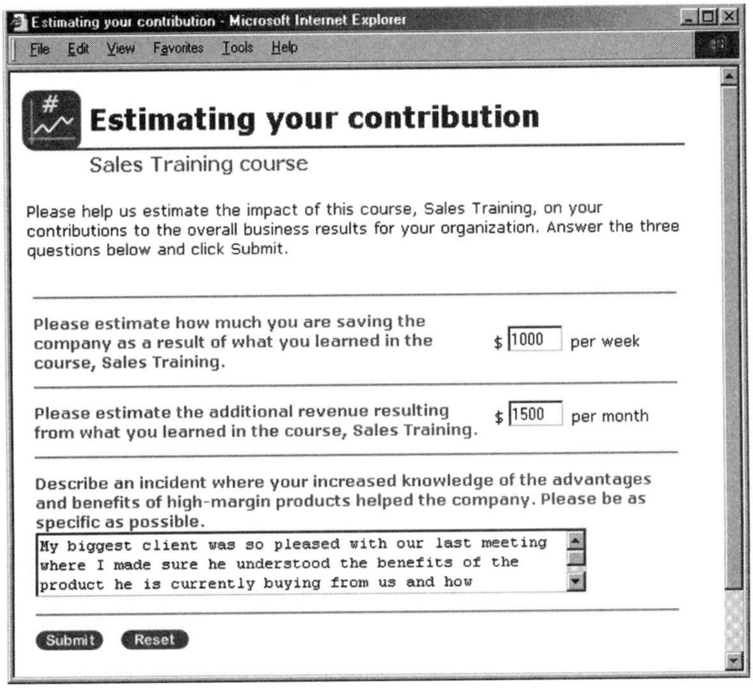

Survey Those Who Should Know

Often the people who take or purchase training are in a good position to at least estimate the business results of training. Figure 6-2 offers some survey questions to ask.

YOUR TURN

Level 4 evaluation connects learning to organizational goals and translates it straight to the bottom line. Nevertheless, business results are hard to measure and even harder to attribute to training.

Can any existing measures of business success be used to evaluate e-learning in your organization? How will you isolate the effects of training from other factors? Answer these questions using worksheet 6-1.

Worksheet 6-1. Can you use existing measures for level 4 evaluation?		
Measure of Business Results	**Suitable for E-Learning? (Yes/No)**	**How Will You Isolate the Effects of Training?**
Sales or revenue		
Profit margin		
Market share		
Stock price		
Customer satisfaction ratings		
Other:		
Other:		
Other:		

What method does your organization's management use to evaluate the financial attractiveness of internal projects like e-learning? How can these measures be adapted to accurately measure the results of e-learning? Explore further using worksheet 6-2.

Worksheet 6-2. Which formula does your management use?		
Formula for Evaluating Potential Investments	**Suitable for Your E-Learning? (Yes/No)**	**How to Adapt to Measure E-Learning Results?**
ROI		
Benefit-cost ratio		
Net present value		
Time to payback		
Learners to payback		
Other:		
Other:		
Other:		

7

Calculating Return-on-Investment

Because ROI is so widely used to evaluate the business success of large, complex projects like e-learning, this chapter is devoted to explaining the technique of calculating ROI. You will walk through a basic calculation of ROI for a training project.

THE BASIC FORMULA FOR ROI

The basic formula for calculating ROI is quite straightforward. You just subtract costs from benefits, divide that difference by costs, and then multiply the result by 100:

$$\text{Return on Investment} = \frac{\text{Benefits} - \text{Costs}}{\text{Costs}} \times 100$$

The term {benefits minus costs} represents the return on the project. The investment is the costs of the project or at least the up-front costs. You multiply by 100 simply to convert the results from a fraction to a percentage.

Say, for example, that you have a project that costs $200,000 but has benefits of $300,000. The return for such a project would be the benefits minus the costs, or $100,000. Dividing this number by costs ($200,000) yields a figure of 0.5, which, when multiplied by 100, gives you a ROI figure of 50%.

THE SCENARIO

Let's look at the process of calculating ROI for training. This calculation is moderate in its complexity, and the numbers have been rounded to simplify the math.

Gizbotics International has a problem. It needs to increase sales of higher-margin products. The chief executive officer (CEO) has set a goal of increasing sales of such higher-margin products by 30 percent over the next two years. Increases in advertising and sales commissions have not worked. Focus groups of customers and sales representatives have identified the main reason for the failure. It seems that sales representatives cannot translate the highly technical features of these higher-margin products into benefits that apply to individual customers. This diagnosis is borne out by the observation that sales representatives who thoroughly familiarized themselves with the features and benefits of the high-margin products sell on average twice as many high-margin products and the same number of low-margin products as representatives who are less familiar with the products do.

The CEO requests that you evaluate the potential of e-learning and classroom training to solve this problem. The CEO expects detailed figures showing the ROI for the project.

Benefits of Training

You decide to start by calculating the potential benefits of training. Unless they are high, there is no reason to proceed further. Your first step is to calculate the profit per high-margin unit sold. From the sales department, you learn that each unit sells for $500 and that "high margin" means 30 percent. That means each unit sold returns a $150 profit.

Price of high-margin products	$500	per unit
× profit margin	30%	
= Profit per unit sold	$150	per unit

Also from the sales department, you learn that sales representatives sell on average 100 units per year, except for the few very knowledgeable ones who sell at least twice that number. You set your training goal as making all sales representatives as effective as the most knowledgeable. By doing so you will increase the annual profit from high-margin products per sales representative from $15,000 to $30,000 for an increase of $15,000 per sales representative.

	Before training	After training	
Average sales	100	200	units per sales rep
× profit per unit sold	$150	$150	per unit
= Profit per sales rep	$15,000	$30,000	per sales rep

To calculate the total increase in profits, you multiply the increase per sales rep by the number of sales reps, which you learn from the sales department is 100.

Increased profit per sales rep	$15,000	per sales rep
× number of sales reps	100	sales reps
= Total profit increase	$1,500,000	

Because Gizbotics is constantly developing new products and because you want your figures to be conservative, you decide to consider profit increases for only the first year after training. Although the potential of adding $1.5 million to the bottom line seems impressive, you must first factor in the costs of providing the necessary training.

Costs of Training

As a training manager, you know that calculating costs for training is complex. You decide to divide the task into three separate kinds of costs: per-course costs, per-class costs, and per-learner costs. Per-course costs are the costs associated with creating the course, regardless of how many times you teach it or how many learners take it. Per-class costs are the costs incurred in offering the course, regardless of how many learners take the course. Per-learner costs are those incurred for each additional learner who takes the training.

Per-Course Costs. Per-course costs are the one-time costs of creating the course. These are primarily the costs of developing the course. To calculate development costs, start by estimating the length of training required. After some study, you conclude that an eight-hour classroom course could do the job.

But what length should you use for e-learning? Sizing e-learning in hours is not the best measure, but you choose to do so because you know that Gizbotic's management understands what you mean by so many hours of training. You know that several studies have found that e-learning can teach the same material in less time than classroom training, but you decide to ignore those potential savings. You want your estimate to be conservative, and you are concerned that your first e-learning project may need a little margin for error. So, you use the same eight-hour figure for e-learning as for classroom training.

The next factor in development costs is the development time rate. This is the number of hours of development time required for each hour of the course. From prior projects, you know that developing original courses requires about 50 development hours per hour of classroom training. For e-learning, you use a figure four times higher to account for the need for additional material and interactivity to do what the instructor does in the classroom.

One final factor is the development cost rate, that is, the cost of each hour of course development. Past projects required $50 per development hour of classroom training. For e-learning, you double this rate, realizing that e-learning will require more technical and media specialists, some with high hourly fees.

To calculate the total per-course costs, you just multiply the course length by the development time rate and cost rate.

	Classroom training	E-learning	
Course length	8	8	hours
× development time rate	50	200	hours development per course hour
× development cost rate	$50	$100	$ per hour of development
= Total per-course costs	$20,000	$160,000	

The $20,000 per-course costs of classroom training looks quite reasonable compared to the $160,000 for e-learning. Perhaps e-learning is not such a bargain. But let's calculate more costs before giving up on e-learning.

Per-Class Costs. The next group of costs you want to include is the per-class costs. These are the costs of offering the course. The term "per-class" relates more to classroom courses, which are taken by groups of individuals as a class. For your e-learning, you decide to teach the course as one large class with learners working through the course at their own pace but with access to a facilitator.

Your first step in calculating per-class costs is to calculate the costs for each group of students to take the course. These costs do not include the costs such as travel and time off the job incurred by individual learners, just the costs of putting a group of learners through the training.

The first cost you consider is the salary for the instructor for the classroom course and the facilitator for the e-learning course. You decide to use a figure of $800 for each classroom class. You estimate e-learning will require $5,000 of facilitator time over the period the course is offered.

Another significant cost is for travel by the instructor to the site of training. Because training will be conducted in hotel meeting rooms in the various sales districts by trainers based at headquarters, some travel will be required. You estimate an average travel cost of $1,500 per class to cover airfare, hotel, meals, taxis, tips, and other incidental expenses. No travel will be required for e-learning.

You must also add the costs of training facilities. Hotel facilities for training average about $500 per day. For e-learning, the only facilities requirement is space on a Web server. A local application service provider agrees to host your e-learning course for $1,000 over the period the course is offered.

Adding up these per-class costs tells you how much it will cost for each class you conduct. Because e-learning does not require travel or meeting rooms, its costs are significantly less than those for classroom training.

	Classroom training	E-learning	
Instructor/facilitator salary	$800	$5,000	$ per class
+ instructor/facilitator travel	$1,500	—	$ per class
+ facilities	$500	$1,000	$ per class
= Subtotal (per class)	$2,800	$6,000	

To move toward a total, you calculate how many classroom classes you must conduct. You do this by dividing the number of sales representatives you must train by the class size. Past experience indicates that a class size of 20 has provided a good balance between economy and effectiveness. Therefore, you need five classroom courses. For e-learning, you already decided to structure the course as one large class.

	Classroom training	E-learning	
Number of learners	100	100	learners
÷ class size	20	100	learners
= Number of classes	5	1	class

To compute the total per-class costs, you just multiply the per-class cost by the number of classes for each form of training.

	Classroom training	E-learning	
Cost per class	$2,800	$6,000	$ per class
× number of classes	5	1	classes
Total class-offering costs	$14,000	$6,000	$ per class

E-learning is $7,000 less expensive than classroom training, but this amount doesn't do much to offset e-learning's higher development costs.

Per-Learner Costs. The final group of costs to consider is the per-learner costs. These are the costs incurred for each additional learner you must train.

One of the main costs is that of work lost because the learner is not on the job while taking training. For sales representatives this figure can be quite high. The sales department estimates that Gizbotics loses $2,000 in profits for each day a sales representative is not actively selling Gizbots. To get the time cost for each learner, you must multiply this figure by the amount of time the learner will require to take the training. Earlier you estimated that training would require eight hours, or about one workday. For classroom training, however, you must add the time learners spend traveling to and from the training. You estimate that travel will add on average an additional day off the job for sales representatives. As a result, classroom training costs $4,000 per learner—twice that for e-learning, which requires no travel.

	Classroom training	E-learning	
Learner's time cost	$2,000	$2,000	$ per day off job
× time required for training	2	1	days
= Time cost for each learner	$4,000	$2,000	$ per learner

To these time costs you must add additional per-learner costs. One such cost is the travel expenses for classroom training. Another is the additional time required of instructors or facilitators for each learner. Each learner requires the instructor or facilitator to answer questions, grade assignments, and perform administrative chores. For this additional time, you allocate $25 per learner for classroom training. For e-learning, you double this figure because the sales representatives are new to e-learning and may require more encouragement and technical support.

Adding up these individual per-learner costs yields the additional costs per learner.

	Classroom training	E-learning	
Time cost for each learner	$4,000	$2,000	$ per learner
+ learner's travel	$1,500		$ per learner
+ instructor/facilitator's salary	$25	$50	$ per learner
= Subtotal (per learner)	$5,525	$2,050	$ per learner

E-learning is significantly less costly, primarily because it does not require learners to travel to receive training.

To compute the total per-learner costs you multiply the per-learner cost for each learner by the number of learners.

	Classroom training	E-learning	
Per-learner costs	$5,525	$2,050	$ per learner
× number of learners	100	100	learners
= Total learner costs	$552,500	$205,000	

Wow! In this category, e-learning is considerably more cost effective than classroom training.

Total Costs. You quickly add up the separate groups of costs to get a total for the two forms of training.

	Classroom training	E-learning	
Per-course costs	$20,000	$160,000	$ per course
+ per-class costs	$14,000	$6,000	$ per class
+ per-learner costs	$552,500	$205,000	$ per learner
= Total project costs	$586,500	$371,000	

Though more expensive to develop, e-learning is the less expensive way to conduct training, especially when training large numbers of people who would otherwise have to travel to take the training. But is either alternative inexpensive enough to yield an attractive ROI?

Return

Once you know the costs and benefits, calculating ROI is just a few simple steps. First, you subtract costs from benefits to see whether either alternative has a net benefit.

	Classroom training	E-learning
Benefits	$1,500,000	$1,500,000
− costs	$586,500	$371,000
= Return	$913,500	$1,129,000

Both alternatives promise profitable results. To convert these figures to ROI, you just divide the return by the investment. In your case, the investment is the costs for each project.

	Classroom training	E-learning
Return-on-investment	156%	304%

The ROI for classroom training is impressive, but the one for e-learning is spectacular. Imagine getting 304% interest on your savings account! Table 7-1 recaps the process for calculating ROI for Gizbotics' e-learning course.

The Last Word on ROI:
It's Not the Last Word

Although an ROI calculation can go a long way toward measuring or predicting the business results of training, it should never be the final word. Training is a messy business and returns come in many forms, some of which cannot yet be reduced to bottom-line figures. The following chapters will help you round up some of these softer benefits, but, in the end, you must use ROI calculations to inform your decisions, not to make them. In some cases, you may chose to stick with conventional training because the returns are more predictable and safe. In others, further investments in e-learning may be justified because e-learning requires the organization to develop new skills, to capture knowledge in a more tangible and reusable form, and to recruit and retain new talent. All these actions increase the intellectual capital of your organization, though they are hard to capture in an ROI calculation.

Table 7-1. The ROI of e-learning.

Benefits			
Price of high-margin products	$ 500		$ per unit
× profit margin	30%		
= Profit per unit sold	$ 150		$ per unit

	Before training	After training	
Average sales	100	200	units per sales rep
× profit per unit sold	$ 150	$ 150	$ per unit
= Profit per sales rep	$ 15,000	$ 30,000	$ per sales rep

Increased profit per sales rep	$ 15,000	
× number of sales reps	$ 100	
= Total profit increase	$ 1,500,000	

Costs			

Per-course costs

	Classroom	E-Learning	
Course length	8	8	hours
× development time rate	50	200	hours development per course hour
× development cost rate	$ 50	$ 100	
= Total per-course costs	$ 20,000	$ 160,000	

Per-course costs

	Classroom	E-Learning	
Instructor/facilitator salary	$ 800	$ 5,000	
+ instructor/facilitator travel	$ 1,500	$ —	
+ facilities	$ 500	$ 1,000	
= Subtotal (per class)	$ 2,800	$ 6,000	

	Classroom	E-Learning	
Number of learners	100	100	learners
+ class size	20	100	learners
= Number of classes	5	1	classes

	Classroom	E-Learning	
Cost per class	$ 2,800	$ 6,000	$ per class
× number of classes	5	1	classes
= Total class-offering costs	$ 14,000	$ 6,000	

Table 7-1. The ROI of e-learning (continued).

Per-learner costs

	Classroom	E-Learning	
Learner's time cost	$ 2,000	$ 2,000	$ per day off job
× time required for training	2	1	days
= Time cost for each learner	$ 4,000	$ 2,000	$ per learner
Time cost for each learner	$ 4,000	$ 2,000	$ per learner
+ learner's travel	$ 1,500	$ —	$ per learner
+ instructor/facilitator's salary	$ 25	$ 50	$ per learner
= Subtotal (per learner)	$ 5,525	$ 2,050	$ per learner
Per-learner costs	$ 5,525	$ 2,050	$ per learner
× number of learners	100	100	learners
= Total learner costs	$ 552,500	$ 205,000	

Total costs

	Classroom	E-Learning
Per-course costs	$ 20,000	$ 160,000
+ per-class costs	$ 14,000	$ 6,000
+ per-learner costs	$ 552,500	$ 205,000
= Total project costs	$ 586,500	$ 371,000

Return

	Classroom	E-Learning
Benefits	$ 1,500,000	$ 1,500,000
− costs	$ 586,500	$ 371,000
= Return	$ 913,500	$ 1,129,000

	Classroom	E-Learning
Return-on-investment	156%	304%

YOUR TURN

Perhaps you disagree with some of the assumptions used in the example. Or, maybe you would like to see the example more closely resemble your situation. Get out your calculator and have at it with worksheet 7-1. Using the example in this chapter as a starting point, alter figures to see what difference the changes make.

Worksheet 7-1. Modify the example in the chapter, adapting the model as you see fit.

Benefits

Price of high-margin products	$	$ per unit
× profit margin	%	
= Profit per unit sold	$	$ per unit

	Before training	After training	
Average sales	$	$	units per sales rep
× profit per unit sold	$	$	$ per unit
= Profit per sales rep	$	$	$ per sales rep

Increased profit per sales rep	$	$ per sales rep
× number of sales reps		sales reps
= Total profit increase	$	

Costs

Per-course costs

	Classroom	E-Learning	
Course length			hours
× development time rate			hours development per course hour
× development cost rate	$	$	$ per hour of development
= Total per-course costs	$	$	

Per-class costs

	Classroom	E-Learning	
Instructor/facilitator salary	$	$	
+ instructor/facilitator travel	$	$	
+ facilities	$	$	
= Subtotal (per class)	$	$	

Number of learners			learners
÷ class size			learners
= Number of classes			classes

Cost per class	$	$	$ per class
× number of classes			classes
= Total class-offering costs	$	$	

Worksheet 7-1. Modify the example in the chapter, adapting the model as you see fit (continued).

Per-learner costs

	Classroom	E-Learning	
Learner's time cost	$	$	$ per day off job
× time required for training			days
= Time cost for each learner	$	$	$ per learner
Time cost for each learner	$	$	$ per learner
+ learner's travel	$	$	$ per learner
+ instructor/facilitator's salary	$	$	$ per learner
= Subtotal (per learner)	$	$	$ per learner
Per-learner costs	$	$	$ per learner
× number of learners			learners
= Total learner costs	$	$	

Total costs

	Classroom	E-Learning
Per-course costs	$	$
+ per-class costs	$	$
+ per-learner costs	$	$
= Total project costs	$	$

Return

	Classroom	E-Learning
Benefits	$	$
− costs	$	$
= Return	$	$

	Classroom	E-Learning
Return-on-investment	%	%

If you wish, you can download a spreadsheet containing the example from this book's companion Website at www.horton.com/evaluating/. From this same location, you can download and print out more copies of the worksheet for your activity. Play what-if with an example calculation. Experiment with your model. Which factors have a big effect on the results, and which seem to matter little?

Now, evaluate the ROI of one of your projects. You can use worksheet 7-2 as a model. Notice that it has the benefits in a generic form rather than as in the specific example in the text. What kind of ROI does your project offer? How does this ROI compare to the ROI figures of other projects competing for corporate resources?

Worksheet 7-2. Calculate the ROI for your project.

Benefits

Productivity after training		units per person
− productivity before training		units per person
= Productivity improvement		units per person
× value of productivity unit	$	$ per unit
= Value of productivity increase	$	$ per person
× number of persons trained		learners
= Total benefits	$	

Costs

Per-course costs

Course length		hours
× development time rate		hours development per course hour
× development cost rate	$	$ per hour development
= Total per-course costs	$	

Per-class costs

Instructor/facilitator salary	$	
+ instructor/facilitator travel	$	
+ facilities	$	
= Subtotal (per class)	$	
Number of learners		learners
÷ class size		learners
= Number of classes		classes
Cost per class	$	$ per class
× number of classes		classes
= Total class-offering costs	$	

Worksheet 7-2. Calculate the ROI for your project (continued).

Per-learner costs

Learner's time cost	$	$ per day off job
× time required for training		days
= Time cost for each learner	$	$ per learner

Time cost for each learner	$	$ per learner
+ learner's travel	$	$ per learner
+ instructor/facilitator's salary	$	$ per learner
= Subtotal (per learner)	$	$ per learner

Per-learner costs	$	$ per learner
× number of learners		learners
= Total learner costs	$	

Total costs

Per-course costs	$
+ per-class costs	$
+ per-learner costs	$
= Total project costs	$

Return

Benefits	$
− costs	$
= Return	$

Return-on-investment	%

8

Including More Costs and Benefits

The preceding analyses have of necessity been simple. Your project may be anything but simple. To accurately predict and measure its value, you must include all relevant costs and benefits of developing, deploying, offering, and evaluating e-learning. This chapter will help you identify and measure additional costs and benefits of e-learning.

COUNTING HARD, SOFT, AND FUZZY BENEFITS

You can make your evaluations more accurate and plausible by considering additional benefits and costs, especially intangible ones. In your quest for additional benefits to include in your calculations, consider three types of benefits: hard, soft, and fuzzy (figure 8-1).

Hard benefits are easy to quantify and express as monetary values. They are what show up in most analyses. These benefits include things like cost savings, savings in time, increases in production, and improvements in quality. Soft benefits are ones that are difficult to quantify and to express as monetary values. They are often ignored, though they are sometimes quite substantial and worth the extra effort to discover and document. Soft benefits are things not tied to quality or rate of output. Soft benefits include general improvements in work performance, the work environment, and career development and advancement.

Fuzzy benefits are impossible to quantify and express as monetary values. Nonetheless, they may be important for your analysis. Fuzzy benefits are the true intangibles. They are abstractions like satisfaction, initiative, and leadership—things every organization believes it needs but none can accurately measure. Fuzzy benefits also include contributions to basic business skills such as

Figure 8-1. Three categories of benefits for you to consider in evaluation of e-learning.

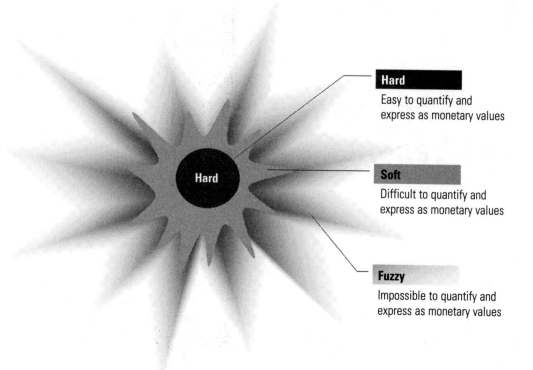

Hard
Easy to quantify and
express as monetary values

Soft
Difficult to quantify and
express as monetary values

Fuzzy
Impossible to quantify and
express as monetary values

writing, speaking, and logical reasoning. Though necessary, such skills are several layers removed from bottom-line figures. Rather than ignore fuzzy benefits or use dubious techniques to quantify them, you may want to list them as extra incentives in your evaluation.

Hard Benefits

Hard benefits are ones easily quantified and so closely linked to business objectives that converting them to monetary values poses little difficulty. Table 8-1 lists and defines some major hard benefits.

Soft Benefits

Soft benefits take some effort to quantify and to convert to monetary values. Table 8-2 explains the three main groups of soft benefits.

Fuzzy Benefits

Fuzzy benefits are intangible factors and take heroic efforts and courageous assumptions to measure and reduce to monetary values. They fall into several main areas as outlined in table 8-3.

Table 8-1. Hard benefits to measure in evaluations of e-learning.

Hard Benefit	Definition	Examples
Direct Cost Savings	As Ben Franklin said, "A penny saved is a penny earned." Any reduction in direct costs results in bottom-line savings. Such savings may be reported as an absolute level, a percentage of total costs, or as a relative change.	Some examples of direct costs that can be reduced include • fixed and overhead costs • cost per unit manufactured, inspected, serviced, or otherwise processed • cost per person served, assisted, or otherwise handled • costs per project or program • cost of sales, operations, or other specific kinds of activities.
Production Increases	Production benefits occur when the same number of people are able to perform more work in the same amount of time. Production increases have their greatest value when an organization has more demand for its products and services than it can currently meet.	Production is measured as: • units created, manufactured, checked, assembled, or processed • items sold, leased, or licensed • forms, applications, or other documents processed • people interviewed, processed, served, or otherwise handled • reduction of backlogs of work, orders, assignments, or cases • turnover in inventory • goods shipped, distributed, or received • transactions completed • accounts opened or otherwise serviced • issues resolved and complaints settled.
Time Savings	Time benefits occur when less time is required for common activities or when time is used more productively. Time savings are most effective in lowering operating costs and getting products to market sooner.	Time benefits can be measured as savings in: • time required for each item manufactured, repaired, shipped, serviced, or otherwise processed • off-job time required for meetings, training, and other not directly productive activities • time lost due to strikes, work slowdowns, and other labor activities • overtime or supervisory and management time • time required to complete projects and percentage of projects or items late • response time or time to complete activities • downtime for equipment and departments.
Quality Improvement	Quality benefits stem from reduced product defects and improving process efficiency.	Examples of quality costs that can be reduced include • product defects and error rates • scrap and waste • rework and repair • accidents and injuries.

Table 8-2. Soft benefits to measure in evaluations of e-learning.

Soft Benefit	Definition	Examples
Work Performance	Work performance concerns how well workers carry out their work and whether they support or hinder others. Work performance indirectly affects productivity and quality levels.	Opportunities for improvement include reducing: • accidents requiring first aid or time off the job • absenteeism, tardiness, and excessive break time • violation of safety regulations or labor rules • failure to schedule absences or call in sick.
Innovation and Creativity	The ability to invent new products and find creative solutions to problems is essential for business success.	Innovation and creativity are difficult to measure but are indicated by: • patents filed • new inventions, discoveries, and developments • novel solutions to long-standing problems • new uses of technologies • new business models.
Work Environment Enhancements	The work environment affects how efficiently and harmoniously a group of people can work together. The resulting effects on morale have far-reaching economic consequences.	Improvements can come by reducing: • employee turnover • complaints by employees • litigation due to employee actions • incidents of workplace violence • labor grievances.
Career Advancement	Career advancement measures the degree to which employees are gaining new skills and taking on increased responsibilities. Career advancement greatly affects an organization's ability to recruit and retain talent.	Measures include • performance appraisal ratings • promotions and pay raises • training programs completed • transfers and training assignments.

Hardening Soft Benefits

How can you calculate the value of soft benefits in hard currency? To quantify soft benefits you must "harden" them so you can measure them objectively and precisely. Then you must convert them to equivalent monetary values.

To quantify soft benefits, start by asking some questions about each benefit. First, how much would someone pay for this benefit? If it were a cost, how much would avoiding this cost save the organization? If you cannot attach direct value to the benefit, can you identify hard benefits that are affected even indirectly by the benefit in question? Does the benefit have any side effects that you can quantify? For example, Amtrak has found that each 1 percent reduction in employee absenteeism saves $6 million per year (Stickler, Bello & Stone, 1999).

Fuzzy Benefit	Definition	Examples
Satisfaction and Happiness	Happy employees are more productive than unhappy ones. Some training interventions therefore aim to ensure that employees are satisfied with their jobs.	Factors that indicate satisfaction and happiness include • job satisfaction ratings • positive attitudes and enthusiasm • loyalty to department and company • self-confidence and esteem.
Initiative and Leadership	Empowered and energized employees take the lead in solving problems and generating new ideas. Initiative and leadership contribute to innovation and creativity.	Some indicators of leadership and initiative include • inspiring and encouraging others • setting appropriate goals and objectives • following through on commitments.
Basic Business Skills	Basic business skills involve the fundamental competencies necessary in any organization for team members to work together productively and happily. Any effort that increases these skills, even as a side effect, will make the organization more effective.	Basic business skills include • listening • making decisions • resolving conflicts • reading, writing, and speaking • understanding business principles and procedures • working in teams • tolerating differences in opinion and approach.

Table 8-3. Fuzzy benefits to measure in evaluations of e-learning.

Is the benefit a stated corporate goal, such as improving market share or reducing time to market, serving the community, preserving the environment, or creating an equitable workplace? You may not be able to quantify the benefit, but it may have considerable power if you can show that your training program furthers a stated corporate goal.

Calculating Monetary Benefits

How can you possibly assign a monetary value to a soft benefit? And, if you do, how can you have confidence in your results? Take a look at the example in table 8-4, which shows how to determine the value of training for resolving customer complaints.

You start with the current level of performance. In this case, you know that before training each sales and support technician resolved about 100 complaints a year. After training, you note that performance has improved by 20 percent, or 20 resolutions per year per person.

You estimate the value of each successful resolution at $50, based on discussions with marketing staff and sales supervisors and managers. Multiplying by the number of resolutions, you see a savings of $1,000 each year from each person.

Table 8-4. Example of how to calculate the value added by training to the resolution of customer complaints.

Current level of resolutions	100	units per year per service rep
× performance improvement	20%	percentage improvement
= Units improvement	20	units per year per service rep
× Value of a successful resolution	$50	per complaint resolved
= Improvement value	$1,000	per year per service rep
× Fraction due to training	60%	percent
= Amount due to training	$600	per year per service rep
× Confidence level of estimate	50%	percent
= Confident improvement value	$300	per year per service rep
× Number of people trained	1,000	service reps
= Total value of training	$300,000	per year

But how much of this savings is because of training? You ask employees and supervisors who tell you that 60 percent of the savings is due to training and the rest due to improved awareness of the importance of resolving problems. This means that $600 of the savings is due to training.

But how confident are you in these estimates? Again you ask supervisors and employees, who say they are 50 percent confident in the assumptions you have used. So, you multiply your savings by 50 percent to get a lower limit—an amount that you are confident is due to training. In this example, this amounts to $300 saved per year per person.

All that is left is to multiply the per-person savings by the number of people trained, 1,000 in this example, to calculate that total value of training is $300,000 to the organization.

Rediscovering Opportunity Costs

Opportunity costs refer to the costs of work left undone and opportunities not realized. Sometimes they are called lost-opportunity costs to emphasize that they stem from unrealized opportunities. In the ROI calculation in chapter 7, you took into account the profits lost while sales representatives were taking training rather than selling products. Opportunity costs can also include inefficiency on the job caused by ignorance, improper techniques, or too much time spent on nonproductive tasks. Another common form is the supervisory and expert time required to correct and tutor untrained employees.

When evaluating training, you most often encounter opportunity costs when you consider the amount of time a person must be off the job to take training. Take the example in table 8-5 of the cost of sales lost during the time a 100-person salesforce takes a four-day course.

Table 8-5. Opportunity cost of time off the job for sales staff.		

Average sales per territory	$20,000	$ per day
× fraction from sales rep	50%	require sales rep
= Average sales by sales rep	$10,000	$ per day
× time off job	4	days
= Sales volume lost	$40,000	$ per sales rep
× profit margin	22%	
= Profit lost	$8,800	$ per sales rep
× number of sales reps	100	sales reps
= Total opportunity cost	$880,000	

You start with the amount sold each day in the average, one-person sales territory: $20,000. Not all of these sales depend on the presence of the sales representative in the territory. Assume that sales drop by 50 percent when the sales representative is not available. That means that each day the sales representative is in training, the company loses $10,000 in sales. For a four-day class, the company loses four times this amount, or $40,000.

That loss is a loss in revenue, but what about profit? Now assume that the company has a 22 percent profit margin on sales. That means that for every dollar of sales, the company makes 22 cents. Therefore, the company loses $8,800 in profit while each sales representative is in training. Multiplying this figure by 100 sales representatives shows that the company has a lost opportunity cost of $880,000 for training 100 sales representatives.

If your training solution reduces opportunity costs, it is a benefit. Suppose that you could reduce the amount of time off the job for training from four days to two days. You would save $440,000 in opportunity costs.

Including Life Cycle Costs

Many financial evaluations consider only the costs and benefits that accrue during the first year. Such a short-term view may distort the true costs and benefits of e-learning projects, which may span several years. To accurately evaluate e-learning, you may need to consider life cycle costs, that is, all the costs over the entire life span of the project. The benefits of training continue as long as trainees are applying what they learned to their jobs.

As an example, figure 8-2 shows the quarterly costs and benefits of a hypothetical e-learning project. Notice that costs are highest during the first year when benefits are still unrealized. Starting halfway through the second year, benefits exceed costs as they do for the rest of the five-year period.

Considering only first-year costs distorts evaluations for e-learning because e-learning tends to front-load costs. That is, most of the heavy costs for e-learning occur during the first year, but its stream of benefits may not appear until following years.

Figure 8-2. Costs and benefits of an e-learning project over time.

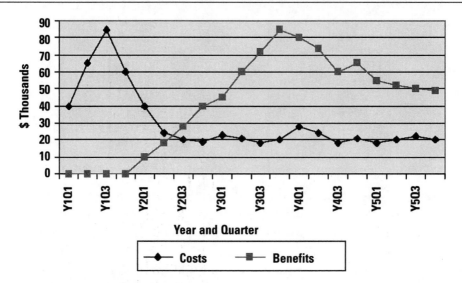

Accounting for the Value of Money

Another problem can occur on multiyear projects if you fail to take into account the value of money. In an era of low interest rates and low inflation, it is easy to forget that a cost or benefit in the future is worth less than one in the present.

Table 8-6 offers an example. It assumes that money is available at 8 percent interest. It tallies the costs and benefits to calculate a net benefit for each year. It then discounts these benefits to restate them in current dollars, not future dollars.

If this calculation seems like financial voodoo, just remember a couple of facts. First, money in the future is worth less than money in the present. The difference in value is the interest the money could have earned between the present and that future date. The formula for discounting future value is:

$$\text{Present value} = (\text{net cash flow in year 1})/(1 + \text{interest rate}) +$$
$$(\text{net cash flow in year 2})/(1 + \text{interest rate})^2 +$$
$$(\text{net cash flow in year 3})/(1 + \text{interest rate})^3 +$$
$$(\text{net cash flow in year 4})/(1 + \text{interest rate})^4 ...+...$$
$$(\text{net cash flow in year } n)/(1 + \text{interest rate})^n$$

Such calculations are complex, but most financial calculators and spreadsheet programs offer them as built-in features.

Sharing Costs Over Multiple Projects

Another source of inaccuracy occurs when you fail to properly allocate the costs of shared resources. In considering the costs of developing a course, for example, you should separate the costs that will be spread over several projects from those unique to each project.

Table 8-6. Calculating the present value of a training project.

Interest rate: 8%

Year	1	2	3	4	5	Total
Costs	$300,000	$20,000	$40,000	$20,000	$20,000	$400,000
Benefits	$200,000	$200,000	$200,000	$200,000	$200,000	$1,000,000
Net benefits	$(100,000)	$180,000	$160,000	$180,000	$180,000	$600,000
Discounted net benefits	$(100,000)	$166,667	$137,174	$142,890	$132,305	$479,036

In the example shown in table 8-7, sharable costs include the costs for a server, design templates, and authoring tools. These total $65,000 but are incurred only once, not once for each course developed.

Table 8-7. Costs that can be shared among multiple projects.

Sharable Costs	Amount
Server	$10,000
Templates	$50,000
Authoring tools	$5,000
Total sharable costs	$65,000
Unique content	**$50,000**

The unique costs for each course total $50,000. If you produce only one course, the cost is $115,000. But if you produce five courses, the cost per course drops to $63,000 (table 8-8). The more courses you produce, the lower your cost per course.

Time Is the Currency of the New Economy

In many highly competitive, rapidly advancing fields, time to market is a more important metric than costs of development. Many management experts suggest that in the new economy, it is more important to get products out on time than to do so within budget. Consider this example of how e-learning could yield benefits in this currency of the new economy: time.

Suppose that products of the hypothetical company Gizbotics currently have a sales cycle of 12 months. That means that after 12 months they are no longer competitive. Before sales can begin, Gizbotics must train its worldwide salesforce on the features, benefits, and competitive advantages of its latest creations. Such training requires the sales training team to travel to eight different locations where the members conduct weeklong, high-intensity training for the salesforce. Even if the team is ready to go as soon as the product is developed, training still takes a couple of months or more depending on holidays and other scheduling limitations.

But, with e-learning, the whole salesforce can be trained at once. The training team engages in a two-week crash effort to develop Web-ready materials. Then over the next couple of weeks, the team conducts live, online briefings and question-and-answer sessions from the base location. By shortening the training cycle from two months to one month, Gizbotics gets the product to market earlier, adding a full month to the sales cycle. The extra month can be expected to add 8 percent to sales just by increasing the time over which the product is sold. The gains may be much greater as the earlier commencement of sales means that the product will seem more innovative and have less competition. It is likely to attract more attention from industry press and boost the image of Gizbotics as the leader in this industry.

Table 8-8. Per-course costs drop if you produce more courses.

Number of Courses	Cost per Course
1	$115,000
5	$63,000
10	$56,500
20	$53,250

YOUR TURN

A sophisticated evaluation requires carefully tallying *all* costs and benefits, including intangible soft benefits. It also requires considering the time span of the project and basic economic assumptions. For your e-learning project, list as many hard, soft, and fuzzy benefits as possible in worksheet 8-1. Which should you include in your calculation of financial results and which should you just mention but not quantify?

Worksheet 8-1. Evaluate all benefits of your e-learning project.		
Benefit of E-Learning Project	**Hard, Soft, or Fuzzy?**	**Include in Analysis or Just Mention It?**
1.		
2.		
3.		
4.		
5.		

Pick a soft benefit that you want to include in your financial calculations and state how you will calculate its monetary value. First pick the benefit and list it in worksheet 8-2. Next decide how you will quantify this benefit.

Worksheet 8-2. Calculating the value of a soft benefit.

List a Soft Benefit:

Technique for Estimating Value	Can You Use This Technique? (Yes/No)	Method for Calculating the Monetary Value of the Benefit?
Estimate costs someone would pay for it		
Identify hard benefits affected by this benefit		
Identify side effects of the benefit		
Connect the benefit to a stated corporate goal		

For your e-learning project, chart on worksheet 8-3 when the costs will come due and when the benefits will occur. Will a lag between costs and benefits be a problem?

Worksheet 8-3. Show costs over the life cycle of the project.

Benefits and costs

Time

9

Consider Both Producers and Consumers

Even projects with a high ROI can fail if their evaluations consider only one viewpoint. Effective evaluations consider the results of training separately for both the producer and the consumer of training. Unless both viewpoints show an attractive return, the project is unlikely to succeed.

Producer's Viewpoint

The producer of training, in this context, is the organization that develops and offers the training. If that organization is a stand-alone firm, then there is seldom confusion. However, if a corporate training department produces training, the proper viewpoint depends on how the overall organization's accounting structure views the training department: as a profit center or as an overhead function.

Training as a Profit Center

If training is viewed as a profit center, then the analysis must calculate costs from the viewpoint of the group producing training. The analysis should include only the costs and benefits experienced by the training group. Benefits or costs experienced by other departments or organizations should be ignored, as they do not affect the profitability of the training group directly. Look at the following example of a for-profit training department or supplier developing and offering e-learning courses.

Costs of Training. First, you consider the costs your training department incurs developing and offering training. You start with the costs of developing the training. For this case study, you assume you are developing 10 e-learning courses at a cost of $150,000 each.

Development costs	$150,000	per course
× number of courses	10	courses
= Total development	$1,500,000	

To these costs you must add the costs of offering the courses over their lifetime. You assume that the cost of offering all these courses is $70,000 per year and that the courses have a useful lifetime of three years.

Offering costs	$70,000	per year
× number of years	3	years
= Total facility costs	$210,000	

Adding up these costs yields a total:

Total development costs	$1,500,000
+ total facility costs	$210,000
= Total costs	$1,710,000

Benefits of Training. The benefits of this for-profit example are the revenues generated by selling access to the courses. To calculate the revenues, you multiply the number of learners enrolled in each course per year by the number of courses and also by the life span of the courses. This gives you the total number of course enrollments, which you multiply by the course price to derive the total revenue generated.

Enrollment rate	1,000	learners per year per course
× number of courses	10	courses
× number of years	3	years
= Total enrollments	30,000	learners
× course price	$100	per learner
= Total revenue	$3,000,000	

Return on Training. Return is calculated by subtracting the costs from benefits. By dividing the return by costs and multiplying by 100, you arrive at an ROI of 75% for the e-learning project.

Total benefits	$3,000,000
− total costs	$1,710,000
= Total return	$1,290,000
÷ total costs	$1,710,000
× 100	100
= Return-on-investment	75%

The spreadsheet for this calculation is available from the companion Website for this book at http://www.horton.com/evaluating/. Try out some different assumptions to see their effect on the result.

Training as an Overhead Function

If training is considered an overhead function, the viewpoint should be that of the larger organization with a full accounting of all the costs and benefits experienced by the whole organization, of which the training department is but a part.

Costs of Training. In this example, the costs of developing and offering the courses are the same as in the previous example:

Development costs

Course development	$150,000	per course
× number of courses	10	courses
= Total development	$1,500,000	

Offering costs

Annual offering costs	$70,000	per year
× number of years	3	years
= Total offering costs	$210,000	

To these costs, add the costs of the time students spend taking the courses. To do so, you multiply the number of learners by the time required for each course, by the number of courses taken by each learner and by the value of learner's time.

Student costs

Number of learners	1,000	learners
× time to take course	1	day per course
× number of courses	5	courses per learner
× value of learner's time	$300	per day
= Total student cost	$1,500,000	

The total costs of training are:

Total costs	$3,210,000

Benefits of Training. Benefits are assumed in three areas: productivity, attendance, and turnover rate. For each improvement, you assume that the organization has calculated the value for each percentage point improvement. To calculate total benefits, you simply multiply each rate by the amount of improvement in each category.

	Productivity	Attendance	Turnover
% improvement	15%	10%	4%
× value of a 1% improvement	$200,000	$100,000	$100,000
= Value of improvement	$3,000,000	$1,000,000	$400,000
Total benefits =		$4,400,000	
(productivity + attendance + turnover)			

Return on Training. Return is calculated as in the previous example.

Total benefits	$4,400,000
− total costs	$3,210,000
= Total return	$1,190,000
÷ total costs	$3,210,000
× 100	100
= Return on investment	37%

Feel free to explore this calculation using the spreadsheet you can get from www.horton.com/evaluating/.

CONSUMER'S VIEWPOINT

Consumers of training are those who decide to purchase or take the training. They include the trainee as well as the supervisor or manager of the trainee. Several large projects have failed because managers forgot to evaluate from the viewpoint of the consumers of their training products. Unless consumers see the value of purchasing and taking a course, the course will not succeed.

Buyers and learners, however, may be on opposite sides of the balance sheet. Many things considered a cost by buyers might be considered a benefit by consumers, or vice versa. Consider the following scenario. A training producer offers a course at a vacation resort. Will consumers view this as a benefit? To the learner, an expense-paid trip to a resort is definitely a benefit, almost like a free vacation. To the boss, however, the expenses of sending an employee to a vacation resort may seem like an expensive boondoggle. Whether something is a cost or a benefit depends on the viewpoint of the consumer (figure 9-1).

Figure 9-1. Benefits are in the eye of the beholder.

Training course at vacation resort . . .

Employees have often regarded expense-paid travel for training as a perquisite or corporate entitlement, especially if the training is held in an attractive location—or a at least a place with more pleasant weather than their work location has. E-learning taken at their desks or at home on their own time may not seem so attractive.

Evaluating Purchased E-Learning Programs

For an organization considering obtaining training from an outside source, the costs of development are replaced by the costs of buying or licensing courses.

Costs of Training. For this example, costs consist of those for obtaining the courses and for the time learners spend taking the courses. The cost of obtaining courses is a simple multiplication of the course price per learner by the number of courses purchased per learner and by the number of learners.

Course price	$100	per course
× number of courses	5	courses per learner
× number of learners	1,000	learners
= Total course costs	$500,000	

To these costs, you add the costs of learners' time spent taking courses. These calculations are the same as in a previous example.

Number of learners	1,000	learners
× time to take course	1	day per course
× number of courses	5	courses per learner
× value of learner's time	$300	per day
= Total learner cost	$1,500,000	

To arrive at a total, you add up the course costs and the learner cost.

Total course cost	$500,000
+ total learner cost	$1,500,000
= Total costs	$2,000,000

Benefits of Training. Benefits are calculated in the same manner as the previous example by adding up effects on productivity, attendance, and turnover.

	Productivity	Attendance	Turnover
% improvement	15%	10%	4%
× value of a 1% improvement	$200,000	$100,000	$100,000
= Value of improvement	$3,000,000	$1,000,000	$400,000
Total benefits =		$4,400,000	
(productivity + attendance + turnover)			

Return. The formulas for calculating return and return-on-investment are the same as in previous examples.

Total benefits	$4,400,000
− total costs	$2,000,000
= Total return	$2,400,000
÷ total costs	$2,000,000
× 100	100
= Return-on-investment	120%

If you want to try out different assumptions, download the spreadsheet from www.horton.com/evaluating/. If you are more interested in evaluating the quality of a course you are considering, see chapter 10, which provides a checklist for quickly assessing course quality.

Enrollment Decisions by Individual Learners

There is no evidence that individual learners who are deciding whether to enroll in a particular e-learning course use spreadsheets to calculate the detailed costs and benefits that apply to them uniquely. There is, however, good reason to believe that these potential learners at least do a mental comparison of the advantages and disadvantages that apply to them as individuals. Table 9-1 lists some benefits and costs that learners may consider.

For successful e-learning, you may need to influence this personal calculation by publicizing the benefits of e-learning and providing resources to overcome fears and disadvantages.

Table 9-1. Some of the considerations that learners factor into decisions about whether to enroll in an e-learning course.

Benefits/Advantages	Costs/Disadvantages
• Obtain job skills needed for promotion or a new job • Please management • Satisfy curiosity about e-learning • Make good use of idle time, such as in a hotel while traveling or waiting to board a plane • Acquire new computer skills, valuable in their own right	• May take time away from other activities • Could spend a lot of time learning nothing • May have to upgrade personal computer or spend time downloading and installing plug-ins • Will require time to learn new computer skills

YOUR TURN

The proper way to evaluate e-learning depends on your economic role and that of your organization. Even an internal department that operates as an overhead cost should understand the business model for e-learning. Such a department does not want its outside suppliers to go broke in the middle of a project. And, trends in corporate accountability may require the internal department to function as a profit center in the future.

Imagine that your organization is a for-profit purveyor of e-learning. Demonstrate the profitability of your operations, plugging your own numbers into worksheet 9-1 and using the example calculations in the chapter as a guide.

What are the main advantages and disadvantages of e-learning-as perceived by your typical leaner? Use worksheet 9-2 to find out.

Worksheet 9-1. Analyze the profitability of e-learning.

Benefits

Enrollment rate		learners per year per course
× number of courses		courses
× number of years		years
= Total enrollments		learners
× course price	$	per learner
= Total revenue	$	

Costs

Development costs	$	per course
× number of courses		courses
= Total development	$	
Offering costs	$	per year
× number of years		years
=Total offering costs	$	
Total costs	$	

Return

Total benefits	$	
− total costs	$	
= Total return	$	
÷ total costs	$	
× 100		
= Return-on-investment	%	

Worksheet 9-2. Analyze from learner's viewpoint.

Main Benefits/Advantages for Your Learners	Main Costs/Disadvantages for Your Learners

10

Evaluating Course Quality

Wilhelmina Loman, vice president of sales for Gizbotics, believes that sales would increase if sales representatives were better at listening to the concerns voiced by customers. She has asked you, as head of training, to recommend a good e-learning course in listening skills. She needs your recommendation in a few weeks; but, of course, offers no budget to pay for a formal evaluation procedure.

A quick search of the Web locates some candidate courses. How can you assess the potential effectiveness of a course without time and money for a formal evaluation? Perhaps the quality evaluation checklist presented in this chapter will help.

WHEN TO USE A QUALITY CHECKLIST

As mentioned earlier, evaluation can have many meanings and be performed in a variety of ways. One of those ways is to use an observational checklist to prompt you to examine specific characteristics of an existing e-learning course. This exercise can help you judge whether the course will meet your needs.

This chapter presents such a checklist. It is short and simple. Though it cannot guarantee that a highly rated course will succeed and a lowly rated one will fail, it can guide you to look more closely at the course and how well it fits your learning goals, your learners, your organization's training strategy, and the subject matter you need to teach.

Before Examining the Course

Before you start examining courses, take a few minutes to recall a few facts about your project that will be essential in evaluating courses:

- What are your specific learning goals and objectives for the training?
- Who are your learners?
- How much do they already know about the subject matter of the training?
- How advanced are their IT skills, especially those required to take e-learning courses?
- What IT (computers, network connections, software) do they have available to take e-learning?
- How motivated are they to learn the subject on their own?
- How proficient are their language skills?
- How many people do you have to train?
- How long do you have to complete the training?
- What are your financial goals for training?
- What is your budget?
- Do you have a target ROI?

Have your answers to these questions reviewed by your management team to make sure you have a consensus.

Examining the Course

Table 10-1 lists the criteria for evaluation and a scoring mechanism. A criterion is a question you must answer about the course you are evaluating. The weight is the importance you attach to that answer. If one criterion is twice as important as another, give the more important criterion a weight twice that of the less important criterion. For criteria that do not apply to your project or do not matter to you, assign a weight of 0. If comparing courses, be sure that the weights are the same for all the courses. The rating specifies how well the course meets the criterion. You can use any rating scale you want, for example, -5 to +5, where -5 is completely inadequate, +5 is perfectly adequate, and 0 is neutral or just barely acceptable.

You can download this form as a spreadsheet (that does the math for you) from the companion Website at www.horton.com/evaluating/.

MAKING THE CHECKLIST WORK FOR YOU

To make this emergency procedure work for you, you must adapt it to your specific needs and resources. Here are some suggestions:

- Add criteria that are important to you and delete ones that are not important.
- Spend time refining the weightings assigned to each criterion.
- Adopt a rating scale, say 1 to 5, -5 to +5, or 0 to 100, that makes it easy for you to express ratings.

Table 10-1. Criteria for evaluating an e-learning project.

Business Issues	Weight	Rating	Score
Do the course's learning objectives match your learning objectives?	_____	x ____	= _____
Are the total costs of the course low enough so that you can meet your financial goals?	_____	x ____	= _____
Can the course be implemented in time to meet your schedule?	_____	x ____	= _____
		Subtotal	
Technical Issues	**Weight**	**Rating**	**Score**
Will the course run on computers learners already have?	_____	x ____	= _____
Will pages and other components download quickly over learners' network connections?	_____	x ____	= _____
Can learners take the course without having to obtain and install additional software?	_____	x ____	= _____
Can the course work under your learning management system?	_____	x ____	= _____
Does the course comply with applicable technical standards (AICC, IMS, SCORM, etc.)? Standards: _____	_____	x ____	= _____
		Subtotal	
Content	**Weight**	**Rating**	**Score**
Is material in the course accurate and current?	_____	x ____	= _____
Does the course cover the subject in sufficient breadth and depth to meet your objectives?	_____	x ____	= _____
Is the course free of production errors, such as broken links, missing graphics, and typographical errors?	_____	x ____	= _____
		Subtotal	
Instructional Design	**Weight**	**Rating**	**Score**
Is the type of course (tutorial, simulation, online seminar, email correspondence) the best choice to meet your objectives?	_____	x ____	= _____
Is material presented in a logical sequence that helps learners understand and master the material? If the learner can control the sequence, is the default or suggested sequence appropriate?	_____	x ____	= _____

(continued on page 90)

Table 10-1. Criteria for evaluating an e-learning project (continued).

Instructional Design (continued)	Weight	Rating	Score
Are abstract concepts (principles, formulas, rules, etc.) illustrated with concrete, specific examples?	_____	X _____	= _____
Do posttests and other assessments adequately measure accomplishment of your learning objectives?	_____	X _____	= _____
Are diagnostic pretests available to help learners custom tailor learning to their individual needs?	_____	X _____	= _____
Is the course certified by ASTD's eCC program?	_____	X _____	= _____
		Subtotal	
Practice and Feedback	**Weight**	**Rating**	**Score**
Are learners given the opportunity to practice ideas and skills immediately after they are presented?	_____	X _____	= _____
Do practice activities exercise knowledge and skills in a way that prepares learners to apply what they learn to their jobs?	_____	X _____	= _____
Are practice activities provided to help learners integrate separate bits of knowledge and low-level skills?	_____	X _____	= _____
Is feedback in practice activities and tests sufficient to help learners recognize and correct misconceptions?	_____	X _____	= _____
		Subtotal	
Usability	**Weight**	**Rating**	**Score**
Can learners get started taking the course (locate it, install plug-ins, register, and access the starting page) using only online assistance?	_____	X _____	= _____
Is the combination of on-screen instructions and online help sufficient for learners to successfully navigate and operate the course?	_____	X _____	= _____
Is it clear what learners should do if they get stuck or have questions?	_____	X _____	= _____
Can learners predict the general result of clicking on each button or link?	_____	X _____	= _____
Can learners take the course without fear of more software crashes, server outages, and misformatted pages than are common with general Web surfing?	_____	X _____	= _____
		Subtotal	

Table 10-1. Criteria for evaluating an e-learning project (continued).

Media	Weight	Rating	Score
Is the text in the course written at a level that learners can fully understand?	_____	x ____	= ____
Is text legible as displayed using default browser settings and only default fonts?	_____	x ____	= ____
Are graphics (illustrations, photographs, graphs, diagrams, etc.) used appropriately, for example, to communicate visual and spatial concepts?	_____	x ____	= ____
Are multimedia content modules used where simple words and pictures are not adequate?	_____	x ____	= ____
Do graphics and multimedia assist in noticing and learning critical content rather than merely entertaining or possibly distracting learners?	_____	x ____	= ____
Will the course be accessible to those with visual and hearing impairments?	_____	x ____	= ____
		Subtotal	

Navigation and Control	Weight	Rating	Score
Can learners decide which parts of the course to take, in which order, and at what pace?	_____	x ____	= ____
Can learners control whether and when large media components are downloaded and played?	_____	x ____	= ____
Are navigation and access mechanisms (menus, browsing trails, maps, indexes) sufficient for learners to find specific items of content?	_____	x ____	= ____
Are units self-contained enough that learners can take them out of sequence without becoming confused?	_____	x ____	= ____
Do learners always know where they are? By examining page titles, constantly displayed menus, or other location indicators, can learners deduce their current location in the course?	_____	x ____	= ____
		Subtotal	

Motivation	Weight	Rating	Score
Does the course initially make clear to learners what they gain by taking the course?	_____	x ____	= ____
Does each lesson or other sizable unit make clear to learners what they gain by taking it?	_____	x ____	= ____
Will the difficulty of the course appropriately challenge your learners—not too hard or too easy?	_____	x ____	= ____

(continued on page 92)

Table 10-1. Criteria for evaluating an e-learning project (continued).

Motivation (continued)	Weight	Rating	Score
Is the visual design (layout, color choices, emblems, icons, etc.) one that will appeal to learners initially as well as over the entire period of training?	_____	X ____	= _____
		Subtotal	
Additional Criteria	**Weight**	**Rating**	**Score**
Other:	_____	X ____	= _____
Other:	_____	X ____	= _____
Other:	_____	X ____	= _____
Other:	_____	X ____	= _____
		Subtotal	
Summary			
Total Score			_____
Average of Ratings (for criteria with nonzero weighting)			_____

- Have multiple evaluators examine a course and compare or average scores.
- Never make a buying decision based on just the score of such a simple evaluation. Use the evaluation as a launching pad for further discussion and deeper evaluation.
- As you gain experience with courses you have evaluated, revise your criteria and scoring procedure to incorporate that experience.

YOUR TURN

Though no observational checklist can substitute for actually testing the performance of courses, a checklist can be a quick way to objectively examine a course you are considering buying. To do so, you must first customize the checklist for your e-learning. The checklist presented in this chapter (table 10-1) has spaces where you can add your own criteria. Once you have done that, use it to rate an e-learning course. Or, if you prefer, download the spreadsheet from www.horton.com/evaluating/. The spreadsheet will take care of the math and let you focus on your critical judgments.

Then, have a co-worker or friend evaluate the same course using the same weightings. Compare the resulting scores with your own. Discuss the reasons for your differences. Remember that this discussion may be more important than the actual ratings.

11

Creating Your Evaluation Plan

You've decided what kind of evaluation you need and have sketched out a strategy. Now you must devise tactics to carry out the evaluation. This chapter will help. It steps you through the decisions necessary to plan your evaluation effort.

WHAT ARE THE GOALS OF YOUR EVALUATION?

The first step in creating your evaluation plan is to list your goals. As you do so, keep in mind your perspective on e-learning, especially the scope at which you want to evaluate, when in the process you will conduct the evaluation, and your economic role. You will also need to decide if you want to do an internal or external evaluation. Finally, you will need to decide the level of evaluation to perform.

The decision of which evaluation level(s) to use will largely determine the kind of results you report and the methods you use to gather and analyze data. In planning, it is tempting to say that you want to evaluate at all levels simultaneously. However, evaluating at multiple levels at the same time can prove difficult and yield confusing, contradictory results. In practice, a single plan can cover evaluations on two adjacent levels at most. If you must evaluate on more levels than that, you will probably need to create and execute separate plans.

Even within a single level of evaluation, plan to measure only a few specific objectives. Trying to measure against too many objectives can be expensive and yield inconclusive results.

WHAT IS THE SCHEDULE OF ACTIVITIES?

The exact sequence of activities in an evaluation depends on your goals and perspective. The list in table 11-1 shows the phases and tasks for one evaluation effort. Though typical, this plan may differ considerably from the one needed for your project.

And, as figure 11-1 shows, the tasks and phases are highly interrelated. You may download this plan as a Microsoft Project 2000 file from www.hor ton.com/evaluating/.

Figure 11-2 offers an example of a one-page evaluation plan. It is designed to be synoptic, not comprehensive. Copies of this form are available from www.horton.com/evaluating/.

Table 11-1. Typical phases and tasks for an evaluation plan.

Develop plan

- Set evaluation goals
- Plan data collection
- Plan analysis
- Set budget
- Write up plan
- Have plan approved

Prepare for training

- Recruit learners
- Gather preclass data
- Prepare facilitator

Conduct the training

Gather postclass data

- Gather end-of-class data
- Gather job performance data

Analyze data

- Convert to numeric measures
- Compute statistics

Report results

- Prepare tables and graphs
- Draft report
- Have report reviewed
- Revise report
- Publish report

Present results

- Determine appropriate presentation method
- Prepare presentation
- Conduct presentation

**Figure 11-1. Timeline for implementing the phases and tasks
of evaluation for an e-learning project.**

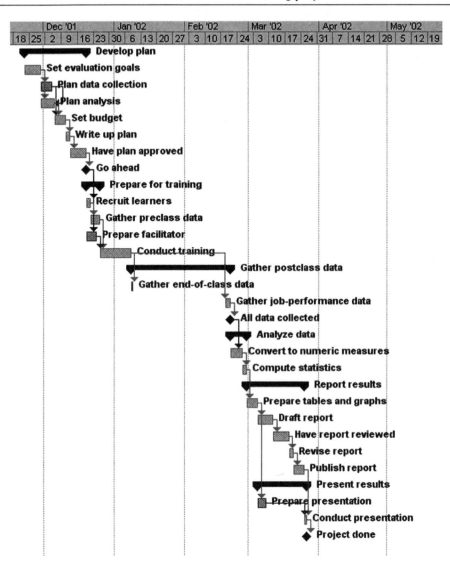

How Much Will Evaluation Cost?

To calculate the costs of an evaluation effort, you can tally the costs of all the individual tasks necessary. For complex projects, you may want to use project-management or resource planning software to help estimate and manage costs.

As a general rule, a complex, full-scale evaluation effort can take one person-year to develop and execute from scratch. Even so, the costs of evaluation should not exceed about 5 percent of the development costs of the e-learning project being evaluated.

Figure 11-2. Example of an evaluation plan.

Evaluation plan — High-margin sales training

ID

Project	Scope	Identification	Page	Owner
Program: High-margin sales training	Evaluation of the first version of the training only.	HMST-Evaluation Plan-01 Version 1.1 - 12 Nov 2000	1 of 1	Copyright © 2000 William Horton Consulting, Inc. 838 Spruce St., Boulder, CO 80302 USA +1.303.545.6604 william@horton.com

Goal

Purpose	Levels	Objectives to measure	Budget
To gauge the effectiveness of the training program in meeting its business objectives.	□ 1 Response ☒ 2 Learning ☒ 3 Performance □ 4 Results	As stated in the program charter: To increase sales of high-margin products by ensuring that sales representatives can translate product features into benefits that customers can understand and appreciate.	$12,000 USD in salary-time of participants

Process — Schedule

Step	Date	Who	Step	Date	Who	Step	Date	Who	By whom?
Specify detailed eval plan.	12 Dec 00	Trng mgr	Analyze data	25 Feb 01	Analysis team				
Conduct training	1-10 Jan 01	Facilitator	Report results	5 Mar 01	Trng mgr				
Gather data	1-8 Feb 01	Trng dept staff							

Data collection

Data item	When?	How collected?	From whom?
Knowledge of high-margin features / Ability to translate to customer-benefits	At start and end of training	Online tests of knowledge of features	Trainees
Sales rate of high-margin products	30 days after trng	Sales figures for products by trained reps	Sales managers
Are customers buying because sales reps are better informed	30 days after trng	Interviews and focus groups	Customers and sales managers

Analysis

Target measures	Methods of calculation	How controlled for other factors	Who performs analysis
Knowledge levels of features and benefits of high-margin products before and after training / Sales increase due to the training program	For knowledge: average and std deviation of increase. For sales, multiply percent of increase thought due to training by confidence in this estimate to yield a confident lower estimate of effect of training.	Trained group will receive no other sources of knowledge. Sales managers and customers will be asked to estimate what percentage of the sales increase resulted from better informed sales representatives as apart from other factors.	Manager of a parallel training department—one with no stake in the results of this evaluation.

Report

What results reported?	To whom?	How communicated
Increases in knowledge of features and benefits / Sales increase due to training	Director of training and VP of HR / Sales managers involved / All training department managers / Sales reps who participated	See below

Form	Format
☒ Paper report	10-15 pages summarizing main findings
□ Online report	
☒ Presentation	45-60 minutes with graphs summarizing findings

WHAT DATA WILL YOU GATHER?

The data you must gather will depend on the specific goals of your evaluation and also on the level at which you evaluate. For example, a level 1 evaluation may gather data on learners' feelings about the course, its content, the facilitator, and so forth. A level 3 evaluation may monitor changes in job performance possibly influenced by training. (See chapters 3–6 for specific recommendations.)

As you list the data you want to gather, remember to include basic demographic data (age, gender, job position) that you will need later to distinguish for which groups your training works best.

Be prepared to make tradeoffs in the data items you gather. If you gather too few items, you may miss important trends and relationships. If you attempt to gather too many items, data providers may fail to complete questionnaires or they may give "robotic" responses. Also, important observations may be lost in complex and lengthy reports.

As a general rule, plan to collect about 10 to 20 data items from each participant.

WHO CAN PROVIDE THE DATA?

To gather meaningful data, ask those who should know. These are the people in positions to accurately comment on the effectiveness of learning. Those who should know may include the following:

- trainees*
- trainers/facilitators*
- supervisors or managers of trainees*
- subordinates of trainees
- peers of trainees
- senior managers and executives over trainees
- customers of your company who interact with trainees
- subject matter experts.

*Be aware that evaluations by the trainee, the trainee's supervisor, or the trainer/facilitator may tend to overstate effectiveness as all have a stake in positive results.

HOW WILL YOU MOTIVATE PARTICIPANTS?

Low response rates to surveys and other data gathering efforts can endanger accuracy or credibility of the results. Repeated reminders to "Please fill in your survey form" can seem like nagging and can generate negative attitudes that remain long after the evaluation process.

The best way to motivate participants is early in the process. By explaining the evaluation and its importance, you can prepare participants to play their roles in the process. For example, figure 11-3 shows an email message sent to the supervisors of learners selected for taking an experimental training program.

As you plan ways to motivate participation, do not overlook such obvious steps as withholding the course diploma until feedback is received or rewarding participants with gifts such coffee mugs or tee shirts.

HOW WILL YOU COLLECT DATA?

Consider the various methods for collecting data and how you can implement them. The following sections describe some common methods. More methods of collecting data are discussed in chapters 3–6, where they are suggested for gathering data for a particular level of evaluation.

Survey Questionnaires

Survey questionnaires offer a relatively economical way to gather data from a statistically significant number of people. Use survey questionnaires to gather

---

Figure 11-3. Using email to motivate participation in the evaluation process.

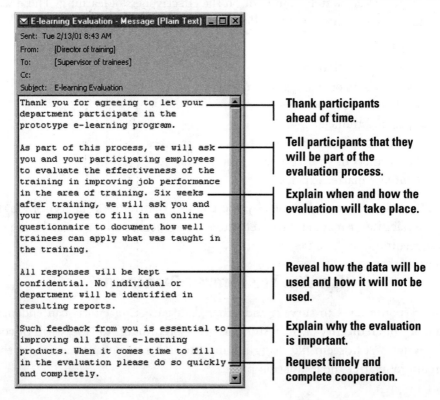

broad baseline data. They are especially good for gauging opinions and gathering demographic data, provided participation is broad and balanced. If completion rates are low, survey questionnaires may not accurately represent the group surveyed.

Survey questionnaires are traditionally administered using paper forms. The data is hand-transcribed and tallied. Online forms can automate much of the work of conducting surveys. Forms can be emailed to participants who can answer right on the screen. Their answers can be automatically entered in a database and summary reports generated. Online forms, however, may skew results toward the views of those who are most comfortable with Web technologies.

Interviews With Those Who Should Know

Interviews use specific, but open-ended, questions of individuals who are in positions to accurately gauge the effectiveness of training. Interviews let individuals express ideas fully. Follow-up questions and observations of body language or tone of voice can clarify ambiguous answers. Interviews can explore ideas surfaced by the interviewee.

Use interviews for open-ended questions for which the emotional response is as important as the words spoken by the interviewee. Interviews, however, are time-consuming, and the quality of the results depends on the skill and personality of the interviewer.

Traditionally conducted in face-to-face meetings or by telephone, interviews can also be conducted by chat sessions or videoconferencing, provided that interviewees have the necessary technology and are comfortable using it. Of the two alternatives, chat is the weakest. It allows no observation beyond the words of the participant. And, participants must be fluent typists to maintain the flow of ideas. Chat does, however, produce a text transcript of the conversation.

Focus Groups

Focus groups bring together knowledgeable participants to answer questions and discuss the issues being researched. In focus groups, participants can hear and comment on each other's observations. Focus groups can reveal ideas and feelings that may not come to light during interviews. Furthermore, they can be efficient, as they do not require conducting many separate interviews. Use focus groups to gauge general sentiment on an issue and to brainstorm ideas for solving a problem.

On the other hand, gathering the required number of people can prove expensive and difficult to schedule. Unless carefully managed, groups can lose focus and stray to irrelevant subjects, yielding data that is useless.

Focus groups are traditionally conducted in face-to-face meetings in a conference room. Sometimes they are audio- or videotaped. If getting the required people together in one place proves difficult, consider using electronic conferencing technology. A conference call may work for small groups. Otherwise, use online meeting software. Chat, videoconferencing, shared screens, and whiteboards provide ways for distant participants to share ideas. Before the meeting, though, make sure participants are comfortable with the technology.

Online discussion forums or computer bulletin boards are also useful for focus groups, especially if it is not practical for participants to be online at the same time or if participants need time to consider their own comments and those of others.

Observation

To see whether individuals can successfully perform a skill, you can simply observe their attempt. Observing performance removes doubt as to whether someone can perform a required task, follow a procedure, or react appropriately to a difficult situation. Observation is appropriate for evaluating complex performance that involves more than knowledge of the steps, requires subtle judgment to gauge success, and involves great expense if performance does not meet standards.

Direct observation, however, can be extremely expensive because it requires a trained observer at the exact place and time where the behavior is to be performed. It is also subject to the "Hawthorne effect," discovered in a series of experiments that were conducted from 1927 to 1932 by Harvard Business School professor Elton Mayo at the Western Electric Hawthorne factory in Chicago. The experiments measured productivity changes in response to changes in the work environment. Each change produced an improvement—including changes that reversed earlier changes. Huh? What Dr. Mayo discovered is that observing human behavior tends to modify that behavior—and obscure the causes of any changes.

Observation usually occurs in face-to-face meetings where body motions and facial expressions are apparent. For activities performed over the telephone, such as sales calls, the observation can be done, with permission of participants, by eavesdropping on conversations.

Although videoconferencing offers some potential for observing performance remotely, the quality of most desktop videoconferencing systems and their limited availability rule them out in most cases.

Some designers are turning to computer simulations to monitor performance. The learner is observed performing the required behavior in a simulated environment. In some cases, simulations are not as effective as observing in a real environment, but others, such as flight simulators, can be much safer and more economical to stage. In addition, the learners can be observed in scenarios involving mechanical failure or other situations that would not often be encountered on the job. Computer simulations for monitoring job performance need not cost millions, but they must simulate the essential factors of job success.

Tests

Tests are an established and familiar way to measure knowledge. Instructional designers know how to write valid tests, and learners are accustomed to taking them. Simple tests can measure knowledge, but they cannot tell whether the learner will actually apply that knowledge back on the job. Tests are better for exact and explicit forms of knowledge than they are for vague, implicit knowledge. So, use tests to measure knowledge of specific facts, concepts, beliefs, procedures, and processes.

For hundreds of years, tests have been conducted by handing out lists of questions and requiring learners to write their answers on paper. The Web has updated testing by making it possible to administer tests on the learner's screen. The learner answers questions by clicking, typing, dragging, and dropping. Simple questions can be automatically scored and recorded. Nevertheless, you are left with the problem of how to be sure that the person who completed the test is the one registered in the course.

Oral exams, in which an examiner asks learners questions aloud, can also be implemented electronically, either by telephone, chat session, or other form of online conferencing.

Examination of Records

Many organizations routinely record data on job and business performance. These records can be valuable indicators of the accomplishment of training objectives. Basing training evaluations on data already recorded by the organization can save the costs of collecting and aggregating data. This practice can also help keep the training evaluation focused on metrics already acknowledged as important to the organization.

Existing job and business performance data may not relate strongly to training success. Such measurements may be influenced by many factors unrelated to training. Use job and business performance data when the measures directly relate to the goals of training.

If possible, obtain business data in a structured, electronic form such as a database or spreadsheet. That way you can summarize and combine individual factors to obtain the metrics that most closely reflect the success of training.

WHEN WILL YOU COLLECT DATA?

The timing of evaluation efforts can determine how much you measure and how well the data reflect actual results (figure 11-4). The longer you wait to evaluate, the more cumulative the results you observe will be, but the more those results will be influenced by other causes.

The level of knowledge or degree of application of training can vary during the months following training. Measuring right after training may overstate results for a learning evaluation but understate them for a performance evaluation and miss them altogether for a business results evaluation. An end-of-course evaluation may also miss response data for those who dropped out of the class before completing it.

As you decide when to collect data, keep two principles in mind. First, measure when results manifest themselves. An emotional response to course content or appearance may occur a few seconds after first exposure to a single Web page. Business results, on the other hand, may take months or years to accumulate. In general, the higher the level of evaluation, the longer you have to wait to collect data.

Second, measure and test after equilibrium is reached. Results can be dynamic. Knowledge levels typically decrease in the days and weeks after training. Proficiency, or application, may rise slowly because it may take time for learners to encounter authentic opportunities and to acquire habits of responding to them. The response measured immediately after training may differ from the response measured some weeks or months later, after learners realize how well the training applied to their jobs. You must allow enough time for these dynamic effects to stabilize or else decide at what time the measurements are most valid indicators of success.

Figure 11-4. Determining when to evaluate.

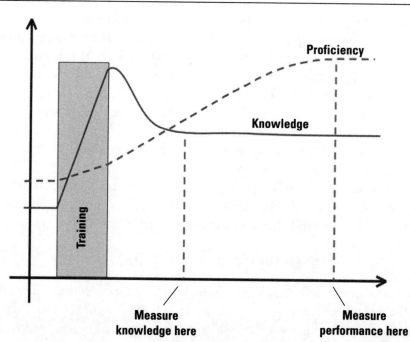

WHO WILL COLLECT THE DATA?

Finding the right people to collect data can prove a difficult chore. True, the job qualifications for data collector are not too restrictive. Those involved in data collection should be objective and unbiased, competent in data gathering techniques, and available when needed. In addition, the required skills and knowledge are not too difficult to learn, especially if the process is automated and if critical procedures, such as conducting interviews, are carefully scripted. Nevertheless, it is sometimes difficult to find enough people available at the right time. Candidates for carrying out data collection include

- instructors/facilitators*
- instructional designers*
- product-support staff
- quality control staff
- marketing staff
- temporary workers from an outside agency.

*Because instructors, facilitators, and designers have a stake in the outcome, they should be used only for collecting objective data. People who have no stake in the outcome of the evaluation should collect opinions and other data open to subjective interpretation.

WHO WILL ANALYZE THE DATA?

A small team with the necessary credibility and skills should analyze the data. The team should be familiar with the goals of the evaluation process and with general techniques used to evaluate e-learning. Skills include common data analysis techniques such as basic statistical functions and charting techniques. The statistical functions used are usually just simple averages, standard deviations, and simple correlations.

The manager or main instructional designer of the e-learning project often performs analysis. However, this can pose a bit of an ethical conflict as these individuals may have a stake in the outcome. In this case, you may want to have the analysis performed (or just audited) by a manager or instructional designer from another department with no direct stake in the results.

HOW WILL YOU ANALYZE THE DATA?

Once you have gathered your data, you must analyze it systematically to see what conclusions, trends, and patterns it reveals. In planning your analysis phase, make sure you answer these questions:

- Which items will you analyze and which will you just report as raw data?

- How will you aggregate and generalize the data?
- Which statistical measures will you calculate and which are necessary to test the validity of your conclusions?
- Which statistical measures will be most meaningful to those who read your report?
- How will you measure and quantify fuzzy benefits (intangibles)?
- How will you harden soft benefits, that is, convert measures to monetary values if necessary?

HOW WILL YOU ISOLATE THE EFFECTS OF TRAINING?

Usually the forces that give rise to a training intervention trigger other interventions and increase awareness of the problem training is designed to address. These other factors may play a role in performance results. Plan how you will separate their effects from those of training.

For example, for sales training, you may need to monitor factors such as advertising placements, price discounts and rebates, sales commission rates, actions by competitors, related product announcements, and general emphasis and attention to sales of the product. Common techniques for isolating the effects of training include the following:

- using control groups who do not receive training but who are equivalent in all other ways
- applying trend-line analysis to identify how prevailing trends were altered by training
- having "those who should know" estimate the effect due to training and their confidence in that estimate.

HOW WILL YOU REPORT RESULTS?

What will be the visible result of your evaluation? Will you publish a report, hold a briefing, or both? And, will you present results as a summary table, bullet lists, charts, or just an executive summary?

If you publish a report, you must consider how much detail to include and in what form to publish it. Will you publish the report on paper, in an online form, or both?

Who will have access to the results? Who will automatically receive copies of the report? Who gets prerelease review copies of the report? Who will be invited to the briefing? Who else can have access to the report or briefing if requested?

Do not overlook the political ramifications of such decisions. Are there any within your organization who may be embarrassed or feel threatened by the results? What can you do to head off any negative reactions?

YOUR TURN

Creating your evaluation plan requires making specific tactical decisions about who will do what, when, and how. Before beginning your evaluation efforts, write a detailed plan, have it approved, and share it with all participants. Use worksheet 11-1 as a guide, or download a blank copy of the form from the companion Website at www.horton.com/evaluating/.

Worksheet 11-1. Plan your evaluation.

Goal of Your Evaluation

Project

Project goal

Level of evaluation required
- ☐ 1. Response
- ☐ 2. Learning
- ☐ 3. Performance
- ☐ 4. Business results

Objectives to measure

Schedule of Activities

Step	Date due	Person responsible	Done? ✔

Estimated Cost of the Evaluation

Data Collection Scheme

Data collected	When collected	How collected	From whom?	By whom?

Worksheet 11-1. Plan your evaluation (continued).

Analysis Scheme

What measures will you calculate?	How will you perform the calculation?	How will you isolate the effects of training?	Who will perform the analysis?

Reporting Scheme

Result you will report	To whom?	In what format?

12

Building Evaluation Into the Development Process

A glance at the rightmost block in the schematic diagram of most instructional design methodologies may suggest that evaluation is something you worry about only at the end of the project. If, however, you want to make evaluation an integral and natural part of e-learning, you may need to rework the beginning steps in your development process. Successful projects tend to be ones that consider evaluation from the start, not just in hindsight.

Because e-learning represents a fresh start, you have an opportunity to build evaluation right into the development process. Doing so requires that you first align the goals of the project to those of the organization sponsoring its development—a good idea for any form of training.

IDENTIFY BUSINESS GOALS BEHIND TRAINING

You probably write learning objectives for your training courses. Ask yourself about the business goals these learning objectives support (figure 12-1). For example, suppose you have a learning objective that requires sales representatives to be able to answer at least half of a customer's questions on the spot without having to consult external materials. Why have you set such an objective? Perhaps it is to support the business goal of closing more sales on the first contact with a customer.

Consider another example: A course on conflict resolution may have as an objective, "convincing supervisors of the importance of quickly resolving disputes among subordinates." Why? To support a business goal of reducing the turnover that results when employees quit the company over disputes with peers.

A course in quality control may aim to teach inspectors how to spot 98 percent of all welding defects. Why? Spotting welding defects can help achieve

Figure 12-1. Each learning objective must originate in a recognized business goal.

Business goal		Learning objective
Close 15% more sales on the first meeting	→	Be able to answer 50% of the customer's questions without consulting external materials
Reduce turnover due to disputes with peers by 80% within a year	→	Believe that disputes among subordinates should be resolved quickly
Reduce repair costs due to welding defects by two standard deviations	→	Be able to spot welding defects with 98% accuracy

the business goal of reducing the costs of repairing welding defects after products are shipped to customers.

By focusing on business goals, we can identify opportunities for training—e-learning or any other form of training—to contribute to the profit of the organization.

FROM BUSINESS GOALS TO LEARNING GOALS

Of course, your training will be more effective if you start with business goals in the first place and derive appropriate training objectives from them. For each business goal, a management team with representatives from training can explore ways to accomplish the business goal. Some solutions may include a business component, an information component, and a training component. The training component gives rise to a specific learning goal (figure 12-2).

For example, the business goal of increasing sales of optional product features by 30 percent may lead to a solution that involves boosting sales commissions for such products (the business component), posting updated data sheets on the product Website (the information component), and conducting training on the optional features (the training component). The first step in accomplishing the training component is to state it as a specific learning goal that is easily evaluated and firmly anchored to the business needs of the larger organization.

SET CLEAR LEARNING GOALS

To be effective, goals must be clear. For evaluation, they must be specific. To set clear learning goals, specify who will do what. Spell out which group of

---

Figure 12-2. Business goals should be the foundation for your learning goals.

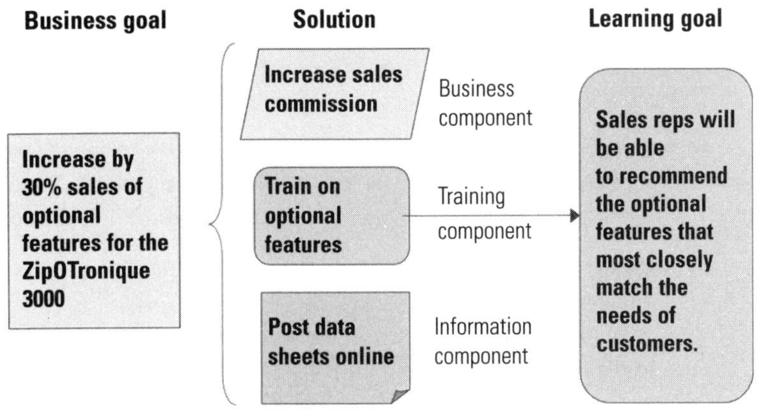

| Business goal | Solution | Learning goal |

Increase sales commission — Business component

Train on optional features — Training component

Post data sheets online — Information component

Increase by 30% sales of optional features for the ZipOTronique 3000

Sales reps will be able to recommend the optional features that most closely match the needs of customers.

---

learners will be affected and how (figure 12-3). As a result of training, what action will they take, what action will they be able to do, what emotion will they feel, what claim will they believe, or what concept will they understand?

Figure 12-3. A simple formula for developing learning objectives.

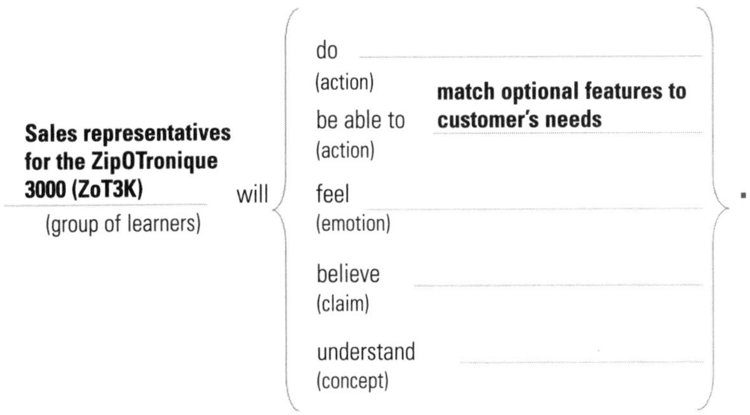

Sales representatives for the ZipOTronique 3000 (ZoT3K) _____ will
(group of learners)

do _____
(action)

be able to   **match optional features to customer's needs**
(action)

feel _____
(emotion)

believe _____
(claim)

understand _____
(concept)

Transform Goals Into Objectives

Goals, even specific ones, are often difficult to measure unless you add qualifying criteria to turn them into true objectives. The goal specifies the person and the result he or she will achieve. For an objective, you add criteria to spell out under what conditions the results are accomplished and to what degree of success (figure 12-4).

Figure 12-4. Converting goals to objectives.

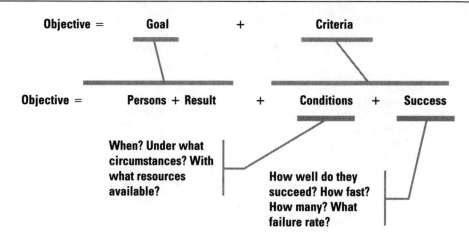

The resulting objective is specific enough that you should have little trouble devising ways to measure it. For an example, see table 12-1.

Table 12-1. An example of a learning objective.

Person	Result	Conditions	Success
What group of learners?	*What must they do, learn, feel, believe, or understand?*	*In what circumstances? With what resources?*	*Time required? Percentage successful?*
Sales reps for the ZipOTronique 3000	Match customer needs to optional features that meet those needs	In face-to-face meetings and telephone conversations with customers Without access to written or online materials	90% of sales reps will recommend the optional features that best match customer needs

STRESS CONCRETE PERFORMANCE

Whenever possible, stress concrete performance rather than abstract knowledge, especially for higher-level objectives. Replace the vague form of traditional educational objectives with crisp performance objectives (table 12-2).

Table 12-2. Words that distinguish performance objectives from educational objectives.

Words Used in Educational Objectives	Words Used in Performance Objectives
Recall	Do
List	Decide
Describe	Plan
Know	Manage
Understand	Complete
Remember	Create

The problem with traditional educational objectives is that they seldom measure the things that matter. Few people get paid to recall, list, see, and so forth. Has anyone ever jumped out of bed exclaiming, "Oh boy, today I'm going to learn to recall the five advantages of the ZottoBopper 3000"? No, people get paid to do work, and they want to learn to do it better.

SET ALL LEVELS OF OBJECTIVES

To integrate evaluation into your project, start with the objective-setting phase. Set objectives in a logical cascade from the highest to the lowest level (figure 12-5).

Figure 12-5. The cascade of project objectives.

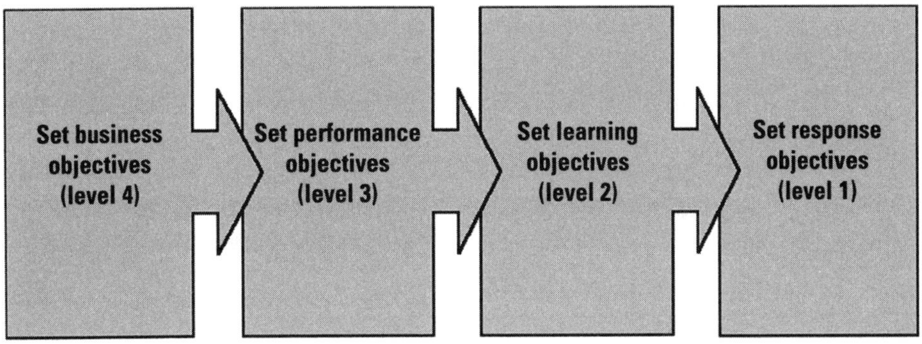

Set business objectives (level 4) → Set performance objectives (level 3) → Set learning objectives (level 2) → Set response objectives (level 1)

The formula is simple: To meet the level n objective, ask what objectives must first be met at level $n-1$. Here's how you can go about it:

1. List your business (level 4) objectives.
2. List on-the-job performance changes necessary to accomplish these business objectives (level 3).
3. List items that workers must learn to make the necessary performance changes (level 2).

4. List the responses necessary for the learning to take place (level 1).
5. Decide which of these objectives your project will meet and which may require other efforts.
6. Finally, decide how to measure the accomplishment of each objective. Figure out which data you must gather and from whom.

YOUR TURN

To make evaluation an integral part of your development process, start each project with easily evaluated objectives stemming from the business goals of your organization. For some of your existing training courses, list on worksheet 12-1 the main learning objectives for each course and the underlying business goal that made training necessary.

Worksheet 12-1. What are the business goals behind your training?

Learning Objective	Underlying Business Goal

For an upcoming training project, record in worksheet 12-2 the learning objectives for business results, performance, learning, and response.

Worksheet 12-2. Set all levels of objectives for an upcoming e-learning project.

Project:	
Business Objectives	
Performance Objectives	
Learning Objectives	
Response Objectives	

13

Pragmatics and Professionalism

Evaluating e-learning can take on a life of its own. The quest for precision can make jousting at windmills look like rational corporate behavior. An out-of-control evaluation effort can gobble up resources that could be better spent improving courses. This chapter concludes the book with suggestions on how to make your evaluation as valuable as possible.

GET REAL AND STAY THAT WAY

To have value, your evaluation must be more than a numbers game. Numbers are of value only if they describe and predict reality. To avoid the pitfalls that trap naïve and hasty project managers, you must understand the requirements and limits of meaningful accuracy.

Whatever you do in your analysis, do not promise more accuracy than you can deliver. A detailed analysis implies to most managers and executives that your real results will exactly match your predicted results. Such managers and executives may even expect a follow-up measurement of results at exactly the same level of detail.

MEASUREMENT IS NOT EVALUATION

Merely collecting and reporting data does not in itself place a value on anything. Evaluation requires saying what the data means. Because technology makes collecting, aggregating, analyzing, and reporting data so easy, it is tempting to overwhelm data-givers with too many questions and to flood reviewers with lengthy reports they never get around to reading.

PRECISION IS NOT ACCURACY

One common blind spot is the confusion of precision with accuracy. Just because you can calculate a factor to five decimal places does not ensure that your result accurately reflects anything in the real world. Just remember that the precision of the prediction is not the same thing as the accuracy of the results. And, often there are tradeoffs between the two. Beyond a certain point, making the study more precise and detailed may make its predictions less accurate.

SENSITIVITY-TEST YOUR ASSUMPTIONS

One way to make your evaluation more efficient and effective is to test your model. Once you have created your spreadsheet or other mathematical model, perform what is called a sensitivity analysis on it. Sophisticated methods are available for sensitivity-testing mathematical models, but the following procedure should suffice for most e-learning evaluations.

First, vary each factor in your model. Factors include values drawn from real-world data and assumptions you are making.

Set each factor in your model to a high, low, and likely value. The high value is the highest value this factor could have. The low is its lowest possible value. For a likely value, plug in your best consensus estimate of the actual value. If you are a spreadsheet wizard, you can set up scenarios to test every possible combination of all three estimates. A more modest approach is to set all factors to their likely value and then, one at a time, set each to its high and low values.

Understate, Don't Exaggerate

While conducting studies on e-learning's ROI, I encountered a new problem, one I had never experienced in 30 years of business life: ROI figures that were too high! Unfortunately, a ROI figure that is too high may lack credibility.

What is too high? The answer depends on your business. If you are in a stable, steadily growing business, executives are used to seeing ROI figures of 25 to 50 percent. A promise of a 500 percent ROI may seem like science fiction—or financial flim-flam. A 200 percent ROI may be more persuasive than a higher figure. Use conservative estimates. Before you serve up your spicy results, consider what your diners are expecting.

Observe which changes affect overall results. Most factors within their low-high range will have little effect on the overall results. Changes in a few factors, however, will have a great effect on the overall result. Focus your efforts on defining these sensitive factors with greater precision. The others, because they do not affect the final result, deserve less care and attention.

PONDER THE ROI OF YOUR EVALUATION PROCESS

Often the hardest part of evaluating e-learning is stopping. Every assumption can be refined. Every formula can be expanded. More data can always be gathered. So how much evaluation is enough?

At critical points in your evaluation, take a few moments to question the return-on-investment of your evaluation. Are all your research, data gathering, and analysis really worthwhile? In one case, according to the Gartner Group, performing a level 4 evaluation cost twice as much as the training it evaluated (Galagan, 2000).

Evaluation should examine costs and benefits fully, but the project should not become an end in itself. Obsessive evaluation can kill an e-learning project just as quickly as a lack of funds can.

SUMMARY: A COST-EFFECTIVE WRAP-UP

How do you know if your e-learning project has a high ROI or is otherwise worthy of the funds and effort lavished on it? If you are teaching primarily factual information or knowledge at multiple locations where learners already have Web access, then the odds are your e-learning project is a worthwhile use of corporate funds.

On any project, calculating and achieving a high ROI begins by defining concrete measurable objectives for the project.

- Learning objectives are not enough. Trace your learning objectives back to the business goals behind them.
- Before you start gathering data, ask the managers who will review your results to approve your formulas and your methodology.
- Spend the time and effort required to calculate costs accurately, but do not obsess over mathematical precision. At this point in history, high precision does not guarantee high accuracy.
- Do not stop with a prediction. Follow up during and after the project to measure actual results. Use actual results to refine your approach and sharpen your calculations.

BEYOND EVALUATION AS WE KNOW IT

Evaluation will evolve and advance. The very technologies that enable e-learning have made new techniques of evaluation practical and made old ones more economical. Newer technologies, such as medical advances that allow real-time monitoring of brain processes, will open the door to more comprehensive and meaningful forms of evaluation.

As the techniques of evaluation improve, the goal of evaluation will grow beyond that of predicting or measuring the results of learning down to the last penny, euro, or centavo. Evaluation will spur innovation and competition by showing us which approaches, theories, techniques, and technologies work best. Evaluation will become an integral part of creative design.

Advocates of evaluation often assert that measuring training results makes investments in learning a sound business proposition rather than an act of faith. Yet until we debug our crystal balls so we can predict the changing conditions for which learning is needed, investments in training will continue to require a measure of faith. But, with proper evaluation techniques, that faith is informed and not blind. We will continue to make mistakes, and we will learn from every one of them. The combination of open-minded design and sound evaluation will ensure that e-learning reaches its potential.

References

ASTD. (2001). *The 2001 ASTD State of the Industry Report.* Alexandria, VA: Author.

Baddeley, A. (1990). *Human Memory: Theory and Practice.* Boston: Allyn and Bacon.

Box, G.E.P. (1978). *Statistics for Experimenters: An Introduction to Design, Data Analysis, and Model Building.* New York: John Wiley & Sons.

Dixon, N.M. (1990). "Action Learning, Action Science and Learning New Skills." *Industrial and Commercial Training, 22*(3), 10–16.

Galagan, P.A. (2000, December). "The E-Learning Revolution." *Training & Development,* 25–30.

Gonick, L., and W. Smith. (1994). *The Cartoon Guide to Statistics.* New York: HarperCollins.

Kirkpatrick, D.L. (1996). *Evaluating Training Programs: The Four Levels.* San Francisco: Berrett-Koehler.

Stickler, G., P. Bello, and R. Stone. (1999). "Business Impact of Amtrak's Right and Ready Customer Service Training." ASTD Annual Conference. Atlanta.

Additional Resources

Binkerhoff, R.O. (1987). *Achieving Results From Training.* San Francisco: Jossey-Bass.

Broad, M.L., editor. (1997). *In Action: Transferring Learning to the Workplace.* Alexandria, VA: ASTD.

Falletta, S.V., and W.L. Combs. (1997)."Evaluating Technical Training: A Functional Approach." *Info-line,* issue no. 9709. Alexandria, VA: ASTD.

Fisher, S.G., and B.J. Ruffino. (1996). *Establishing the Value of Training.* Amherst, MA: Human Resource Development Press.

Fisk, C.N., editor. (1991). *ASTD Trainer's Toolkit: Evaluation Instruments.* Alexandria, VA: ASTD.

Hacker, D.G. (1998). "Testing for Learning Outcomes." *Info-line,* issue no. 8907. Alexandria, VA: ASTD.

Head, G.E. (1993). *Training Cost Analysis: A How-To Guide for Trainers and Managers.* Alexandria, VA: ASTD.

Hodges, T.M., editor. (1999). *In Action: Measuring Learning and Performance.* Alexandria, VA: ASTD.

Horton, W. (2001). *Leading E-Learning.* Alexandria, VA: ASTD.

Horton, W. (2000). *Designing Web-Based Training.* New York: John Wiley & Sons.

Lepsinger, R., and A.D. Lucia. (1997). *The Art and Science of 360 Degree Feedback.* San Francisco: Jossey-Bass Pfeiffer.

Long, L. (1998). "Surveys From Start to Finish." *Info-line,* issue no. 8612. Alexandria, VA: ASTD.

Mager, R.F., and P. Pipe. (1984). *Analyzing Performance Problems or You Really Oughta Wanna* (2d edition). Belmont, CA: Lake Publishing.

Mondschein, M. (1999). *Measurit: Achieving Profitable Training.* Oakland Park, KS: Leathers Publishing.

Nowack, K. (1992). "Self-Assessment and Rater-Assessment as a Dimension of Management Development." *Human Resources Development Quarterly, 3,* 141–155.

Parry, S.B. (1997). *Evaluating the Impact of Training.* Alexandria, VA: ASTD.

Phillips, J.J. (1997). *Handbook of Training Evaluation and Measurement Methods* (3d edition). Houston: Gulf Publishing Company.

Phillips, J.J. (1998). "Level 1 Evaluation: Reaction and Planned Action." *Info-line,* issue no. 9813. Alexandria, VA: ASTD.

Phillips, J.J. (1998). "Level 2 Evaluation: Learning." *Info-line,* issue no. 9814. Alexandria, VA: ASTD.

Phillips, J.J., W. Jones, and C. Schmidt. (1998). "Level 3 Evaluation: Application." *Info-line,* issue no. 9815. Alexandria, VA: ASTD.

Phillips, J.J., and P.F. Pulliam. (1998). "Level 5 Evaluation: Mastering ROI." *Info-line,* issue no. 9805. Alexandria, VA: ASTD.

Phillips, J.J., and R.D. Stones. (1998). "Level 4 Evaluation: Business Results." *Info-line,* issue no. 9816. Alexandria, VA: ASTD.

Phillips, J.J. (1997). *Return on Investment in Training and Performance Improvement Programs.* Houston: Gulf Publishing Company.

Rae, L. (1999). *Using Evaluation in Training and Development.* London: Kogan Page.

Robinson, D.G., and J.C. Robinson. (1995). *Performance Consulting: Moving Beyond Training.* San Francisco: Berrett-Koehler.

Robinson, D.G., and J.C. Robinson. (1997). "Measuring Affective and Behavioral Change." *Info-line,* issue no. 9110. Alexandria, VA: ASTD.

Sharpe, C., editor. (1999). *The Info-line Guide to Training Evaluation.* Alexandria, VA: ASTD.

Tanquist, S. (2000). "Evaluating E-Learning." *Info-line,* issue no. 0009. Alexandria, VA: ASTD.

Waagen, A.K. (1997). "Essentials for Evaluation." *Info-line,* issue no. 9705. Alexandria, VA: ASTD.

About the Author

William Horton has been designing technology-based training since 1971 when, as an undergraduate, he designed a network-based course for the Massachusetts Institute of Technology's Center for Advanced Engineering Study. William Horton created www.DesigningWBT.com, wrote e-learning courses on electronic media, designed a network-based knowledge-management system, and served as a member of ASTD's commission on e-learning certification.

William Horton is an internationally sought-after speaker. He recently delivered the keynote addresses for the Human Resources Association National Congress in São Paulo, the Information Technology Training Association conference in Barcelona, and the Knowledge Management Seminarium in Stockholm.

William Horton is a registered professional engineer, an MIT graduate, and fellow of the Society for Technical Communication.

William Horton is a prolific author. His books include *Designing Web-Based Training, Designing and Writing Online Documentation,* and *Secrets of User-Seductive Documents.* He is co-author of *Getting Started in Online Learning* and *The Web Page Design Cookbook* and CD-ROM. He is also the author of two more books to be published by ASTD on e-learning: *Leading E-Learning* and *Using E-Learning.*

William and his wife, Kit, the other half of William Horton Consulting, live in downtown Boulder, Colorado, just five blocks east of the Rocky Mountains, in a 100-year-old house, which they are lovingly restoring. The kitchen, which he and Kit redesigned themselves, was featured in the April 1999 and September 2000 issues of *Better Homes and Gardens.* You can reach him at william@horton.com.